King Kwong
Larry Kwong
the China Clipper Who Broke the NHL Colour Barrier

PAULA JOHANSON

FIVE RIVERS PUBLISHING
WWW.FIVERIVERSPUBLISHING.COM

Published by Five Rivers Publishing, 704 Queen Street, P.O. Box 293, Neustadt, ON N0G 2M0, Canada

www.fiveriverspublishing.com

King Kwong: Larry Kwong, the China Clipper Who Broke the NHL Colour Barrier, Copyright © 2015 by Paula Johanson

Edited by Lorina Stephens.

Cover Copyright © 2015 by Jeff Minkevics

Text set in Minion Pro, an Adobe original typeface designed by Robert Slimbach in 1990, and inspired by late Renaissance typefaces.

Titles set in Jazzfest, designed by Willard T. Sniffin and Nick Curtis in 1990, and influenced by the typefaces of the Art Deco movement.

Published in Canada

Library and Archives Canada Cataloguing in Publication

Johanson, Paula, 1961-, author

King Kwong : Larry Kwong, the China Clipper who broke the NHL colour barrier / Paula Johanson.

Issued in print and electronic formats.

ISBN 978-1-927400-75-3 (pbk.).— 978-1-927400-76-0 (epub)

1. Kwong, Larry, 1923-. 2. Hockey players—Canada--Biography.

3. Chinese Canadian hockey players—Biography. I. Title.

GV848.5.K86J64 2015 796.962092 C2015-900412-8 C2015-900413-6

Dedicated to my family's own hockey players:
my brother Karl and our dad Joe
and now
Erica with her jersey tucked in
and Johnny B Good

Contents

Chapter 1: On NHL Ice

WHO BROKE THE colour barrier in the NHL? A man whose professional hockey career statistics include leading the senior leagues for scoring and for low penalty minutes — and a single shift on the ice in an NHL game. He was scouted three times by NHL teams before that game, and courted away from the NHL to a powerful role in three different leagues before retiring.

He is Larry Kwong, a Canadian of Chinese descent born in Vernon BC in 1923, a hard-working man and World War II serviceman who played hockey most of his life. He was one of the Smoke Eaters, one of the finest hockey teams in the world at that time. His teammates had factory jobs, but the only work the team could find for Kwong was as a bellhop. He played for two years on the farm team for the New York Rangers, and for years in the Quebec Senior League. Kwong went on to spend years as a player and coach in England and Switzerland where he was a pivotal figure in the development of the Swiss league. Recently, the British Columbia Sports Hall of Fame recognised Kwong in their Pioneer category, and the BC Hockey Hall of Fame celebrated him with their very first Pioneer Award, acknowledging not only his fine career in the senior leagues but also that he played in one NHL game for the New York Rangers. His hockey history is only now being brought again to public attention, sixty years after his 'New York' minute in NHL play.

The Great Game

Larry Kwong's ground-breaking game took place in Montreal against the Canadiens on March 13, 1948. The New York Rangers team had a chance to enter the playoffs that season, for the first time since 1942. With many of their players suffering injuries, the team had to call up players from their farm team, the New York Rovers. Manager Frank Boucher picked two of the Rovers men: left wing Ronnie Rowe and center forward Larry Kwong. Together, the Rovers teammates rode a train from New York City to Montreal, where they would play against a team including hockey greats Maurice Richard and Doug Harvey.

At the Montreal Forum, Kwong put on the blue Rangers jersey with number 11 on his back. "That's what I wanted to be since I was a young boy," he said to himself, as he told journalist David Davis over sixty years later. "I wanted to play in the NHL." He was twenty-four years old, and he was living his dream. Photographs were taken before the game and as the players warmed up.

It was overwhelming to be playing in front of a full house at the Forum. There were almost four times as many people in the stands as in all of Kwong's home town of Vernon, BC. Even so, Kwong was no small-town kid lost in a big city. He'd been playing in Madison Square Garden for two seasons now for the Rovers, and he was fine in front of crowds in any arena.

Kwong was thrilled to be competing with Maurice Richard, a hockey superhero of the 1940s-era NHL, and proud that he would be facing him on the ice. They could end up battling over the puck or facing off, because both players were on their teams' forward lines. "Rocket" Richard played right wing for the Canadiens and Kwong would be filling in at right wing or center for the Rangers, depending upon how the coach would play him. Only two years older than Kwong, the Rocket stood 5" (12.5 cm) taller and carried over 40 lbs. (22 kg) more mass. Perhaps Richard was a slower skater than Kwong — sportswriters called Kwong a "doodlebug on skates." But there could be more power behind Richard's shots. And the Rocket shot left, while Kwong shot right.... If both players were ever on the ice at once, things could get interesting between them. Kwong was ready and waiting to play.

There was time for a photo opportunity before the game on March 13, 1948, showing Larry Kwong in the New York Rangers jersey.

The Clock Counts Down

Once the game began, Coach Boucher put Ronnie Rowe into play frequently, but kept Kwong in reserve. Kwong watched the game attentively from the Ranger's bench as the first period passed without score. The teams were well-matched.

In the second period, the Canadiens scored the first goal of the game. The crowd roared, filling the Montreal Forum with their cheers for the home team goal! Within moments, action resumed on the ice. The Rangers had fallen behind. And still, Kwong waited for the coach to put him on the ice. As one of the leading scorers on the farm team — and in the Quebec Senior Hockey League — Kwong knew it was time to use players who were good at scoring goals. Watching from the bench, Kwong saw the Rangers' little center forward Edgar Laprade skating circles around players on the other team. There was Bill Juzda, the Rangers' hard-hitting defence, and Bill Durnan in goal for the Canadiens.

Late in the third period, the score was tied at 2 to 2, and the teams were deadlocked. Kwong was uncomfortably aware that the last minutes of the game were ticking down, but he waited for the coach's signal.

He was so anxious to play that when Coach Boucher finally sent him out, he didn't wait for the gate to be opened. Over the boards he went and slipped into the game, light on his skates as always. "Finally, I'm on the ice!" he thought. When the puck came his way, he smoothly passed the puck to a teammate.

Seconds later, play was halted briefly by the referee, and before the face-off to resume play, Boucher sent out another player and brought Kwong back to the bench. That was his only shift on ice in an official NHL game. It lasted approximately one minute.

Getting There

Larry Kwong's single minute on the ice in an NHL game was part of a sports phenomenon. The 1947 and 1948 seasons set landmarks in major league sports in North America, as a few professional baseball, basketball, football and hockey teams hired players who were men not of European descent. These changes were not landslide changes. For years to come, there were only a handful of professional athletes in any major league sport who were men of colour.

In April 1947, Jackie Robinson played his first game for the Brooklyn Dodgers, a landmark baseball game that broke Major League Baseball's colour barrier. He was the first African-American to play for that league since the 1880s. That same season baseball player Larry Doby broke the colour barrier in the American League. Within a year there were several black players in both leagues.

In November 1947, Watsuo Misaka became the first Asian-American to play in the National Basketball Association when he played three games for the Knicks. Though Misaka was the first non-white player for the NBA, this American-born man of Japanese parents felt that race was not a factor when the Knicks cut him from the team so they could pick up a player taller than his modest 5' 7" (170cm).

In the Canadian Football League, Normie Kwong (no relation to Larry Kwong) joined the Calgary Stampeders in 1948. At age 18 he became Canada's first professional Chinese-Canadian football player.

Larry Kwong broke the colour barrier in the National Hockey League in 1948, in the midst of these league-changing events. Even so, change happened slowly in the NHL. It would be ten more years before Willie O'Ree became the first black player in the NHL. It was nearly thirty years before Mike Wong played at center for the Red Wings; the next year, 1989, Peter Ing played goal for the Toronto Maple Leafs. Wong and Ing were the league's second and third players of Chinese descent. Even with the expanding number of teams and players in the league in recent years, there have been only fourteen players of east Asian descent, ever.

How Could This Shift Happen?

How could NHL coaches and team managers make the decision not to use a player from their farm team who was leading the minor leagues in scoring? Hockey fans today still don't understand. Could race really matter more than the player's skill?

Compared with the 21st century, 1948 was a different time — a time when it was legal under Canadian and American laws to discriminate against people based on their race or heritage. This discrimination extended even to the NHL. There was Bud Maracle of First Nations descent, who played for the Rangers in 1931. Possibly a few Canadian players had an ancestor from the First Nations. In the 1940s there was a hotshot player in the Quebec Senior Hockey League, Herb Carnegie, who was undeniably one of the best players on his team, and the league. Born in Toronto, Carnegie grew up to be a fine hockey player. He could play for the Quebec leagues, but one thing kept him from trying out for an NHL team: he was black. In 1948 there were no players of African descent at all in the NHL. None of the team owners would hire them. The team managers and coaches would not even give them a tryout. The first player of colour in the NHL was Larry Kwong.

Though Larry Kwong was born in Canada, when he was born he wasn't considered a Canadian citizen or British subject. Under the law he was considered an 'allied alien.' Until the laws changed during the Second World War, he did not have the rights of a citizen to serve in the Armed Forces or to travel outside Canada and return. In the province of British Columbia, he was unable to vote. And even after his war service gave him those rights, it was still legal to discriminate against him based on his race.

The Whole Story

It's not hard to sum up the single game Kwong played for the NHL, the most exciting and disappointing game he ever played, with the support of his team coach and manager but not the league. People find it hard to imagine today that any hockey player could be good enough to play in an official NHL game, but play only one shift, and never again play in that league. But it really did happen, and it was not just some publicity stunt to promote a radio or television show.

Larry Kwong is far from the only player to play in a single NHL game: there were half-a-dozen one-game wonders during that season, but none with a lasting career afterwards as fine as his. Larry Kwong's single shift on the ice in an NHL game happened for several reasons. It takes some explaining to tell Kwong's story, and there's much more to his story than that one minute.

Chapter 2: A Boy in Vernon

DID LARRY KWONG come out of nowhere to become a professional hockey player in the NHL? Not at all. He started out as a young boy playing small-town hockey. From pick-up games to organized junior hockey in a league, he learned the game the way most players do, with his family and neighbours. Like many NHL players, his talent became apparent even as a boy.

In many ways, young Larry was just like most of the other children growing up in small towns in the Okanagan Valley in southern British Columbia. He played with his sisters and brothers and some of the neighbour kids, went to school, did chores at home and found work to earn a little money. The kids he had most in common with were those like him who grew up in "Chinatown" neighbourhoods, born of parents or grandparents who came from China.

Family Beginnings

It was the gold rush that brought Larry Kwong's father from Sam Yip village in southern China to Canada at age sixteen. Like many economic immigrants, this very young man was looking for 'Gold Mountain' — a place where workers could earn cash wages. In 1882, Canadian immigration officials wrote his Cantonese name,

Ng Shu Kwong or Eng Shu Kwong, into their records, confusing his family name Eng with his given name Kwong. He was one of 17,000 Chinese immigrants who came to Canada between 1881 and 1884, some from the USA, but most from southern China.

Instead of working on the railways as so many Chinese immigrants did, Mr Eng worked the gold fields of Cherry Creek in British Columbia. He never found the mother lode and struck it rich, but there was other money to be made in BC. After the gold didn't pan out well for him, Eng walked from the town of Lumby over the ridge of the Monashee Mountains into the town of Vernon. Eng found opportunities for work in farming, and in time was able to marry a Chinese-Canadian woman from Victoria, BC.

By 1895, Eng and his wife were settled in Vernon where, using his wages from a good job in a lumber mill, he was able to rent a grocery store. He became a partner, and eventually the owner of the business. With this reliable income he was able to afford to marry his second wife, bringing her from China and paying a prohibitive Head Tax. They raised a family in Vernon, living over the family store in the part of town that was known as Chinatown.

A formal portrait shows the Eng family with the first of their many children.

As store owners, the family sold not only dry goods in cans and boxes, but fresh vegetables and fruits as well. They knew many people, and had many friends among their neighbours and among the gardeners and farmers who supplied their store. The sign on the front of their building read Kwong Hing Lung grocery. The name Hing Lung means Abundant Prosperity, and to this day many restaurants can be found with similar names in cities where Cantonese-speaking immigrants have settled.

The Eng family came to be known by the name Kwong from their store's sign, rather than their family name Eng. Their youngest son was named Eng Kai Geong, the fourteenth of fifteen children by two wives. Born in July 1923, young Kai Geong grew up speaking both Cantonese and English, and he took the English name Lawrence, usually shortened to Larry. It was common in the early 20th century — and it still is — for immigrants to give their Canadian-born children both an English first name and a name from their homeland's language and culture. The children often grow up using ethnic names at home, and English first names at school and with other people.

A family photo from about 1930 shows the Kwong family business in Vernon, BC.

Head Tax

As soon as the Canadian Pacific Railway was completed in 1885 with the help of Chinese labourers, the federal government passed laws to restrict immigration from China to Canada. A Head Tax of $50 was imposed on every person of Chinese origin entering Canada. Canadian citizenship was not available to Chinese immigrants or their descendants. In 1900 the Head Tax was increased to $100, and in 1903 it was set at $500 — an amount equal to two years' wages for a Chinese labourer at that time. The law was not repealed until the Exclusion Act of 1923.

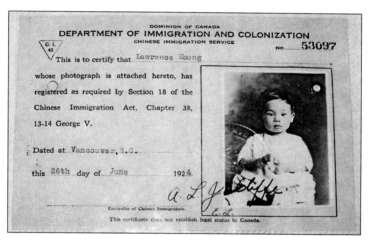

For identification under the Exclusion Act, young Larry Kwong had a C.I. 45 form instead of a birth certificate.

Hard Times

With the death of Ng Shu Kwong in 1928, the family faced tragedy. The eldest children worked hard with their widowed mother to support the family and look after the younger children. When they found work with Chinese businesses in nearby small cities, the eldest daughters sent money home to the family in Vernon, to support the younger children. Larry was only five years old, and Betty a year older, and little sister Ina even younger.

There were no pensions or survivor's benefits available to the family, and with the stock market crash a year later there were hard times for everyone. The world-wide economic Depression had begun, and for ten years it had profound effects even in small towns. There were still natural resources for mining and forestry, but those few jobs were hard to get. The weather was still good enough for farming in the Okanagan valley, but it was hard to earn money to buy the food these farms produced.

Sometimes a package of vegetables would just show up at the back door to the Kwong house. It's a touching memory for Kwong, recalling how his widowed mother was helped by their friends. They shared vegetables from their gardens and small farms, so that she could keep putting meals on the table for the large family.

The Home Team

Like many young boys growing up in Canada, Larry loved hockey. The radio played on cold winter nights, with Foster Hewitt on CBC radio announcing hockey games from the National Hockey League. On Saturday nights in his family's home over their store, Larry listened to the games with his brothers and sisters, following the play-by-play descriptions. They cheered at goals and discussed the games afterwards.

Hockey wasn't just something to hear on the radio and talk about with friends — hockey was one of the most important childhood games. When the streets got icy, that was where the basic skills were learned of skating and stick-handling a puck. Frozen ponds were good for boys playing pick-up games of hockey. Even some girls played a little hockey with their brothers, in casual play. There were amateur leagues where teams of boys could play hockey in many towns. In Canada, a few leagues for girls and young women were formed of teams from universities and schools.

For young Larry, two of his five older brothers were particularly supportive. Jack and Jimmy got him playing hockey. They pushed him to become a good player. As he met obstacles later on, they encouraged him and kept him trying hard. When the weather grew cold enough, Larry's brothers would pour water on the ground in a vacant lot beside the family store and home, making a small, improvised rink.

There was also a pond on a hill above town. During snowy winters, the boys would climb the hill with a shovel. Once the snow was shoveled off the pond or home-made ice surface, sunlight would melt a thin layer that would quickly freeze. This melting and freezing would help to smooth the ice a little, but there were always rough patches.

Thinking back on that pond, it amazes the grown-up Larry Kwong that he and his playmates were willing to walk miles to the pond and back, just to have fun. "We did that then," he said when telling the story. "We played outside, skating for hours at the pond. We got so cold! And one day when it was warmer, the ice went rubbery. It was thawing, and when I stepped on it, I could feel the ice bending. The water soaked up from below. The ice rippled and the movement went across the pond like waves. When I went back to shore I thought, why did I do that? That was so dangerous!"

A candid family photo shows Larry and Betty Kwong and two neighbour boys playing hockey on an icy street.

Equipment

During the years of the Depression, few people had any money to spend on store-bought equipment for hockey or other sports. Like many boys, the Kwong brothers and their neighbours made as much of their own hockey equipment as they could.

Sometimes a pair of boots would be set up as temporary goalposts for a quick game. For shin guards, players would stuff an Eaton's catalogue or folded newspaper down the front of their knee-high woolen socks — and the socks were usually home-knitted. Players were bare-headed or wore home-made hats and toques, because nobody wore helmets in those days. Only the goalies wore much in the way of protective equipment, with an old baseball glove on the catching hand, and sometimes a jockstrap. Home-made knitted mittens, sometimes layered under leather mitts, were a good substitute for store-bought hockey gloves.

It's hard to make a hockey stick at home that works as well as the commercial sticks. But someone who is handy can repair a broken blade on a stick. Even little kids could learn to help repair sticks or modify the blade to keep it strong.

"We would tape the blade with black electrical tape," explained Kwong. "We would take an empty can of salmon, wash it and flatten it, and slip it over the blade. Then we wound tape around it. That would keep the blade from breaking. The hockey sticks would last longer!"

Players had to make their sticks last. While a professional team could buy sticks wholesale at $2 each, in the 1930s it could cost $3 to buy one stick. That was an entire day's pay for a man working a good job at a lumber mill.

A hockey puck is a disc of tough rubber that can last for years of rough play. But if you didn't have a hockey puck for your casual games, it didn't matter. Some kids would use a rubber ball, even though it rolled rather than sliding on the ice. Others whittled pucks out of wood and burnt them black on top of a woodstove, but found wood was much lighter than a rubber puck.

"Even if you had a puck," as Kwong pointed out in conversation, "someone would make a wild hit and it could fly into a snowdrift and be lost." On the icy streets, another alternative was available — frozen horse droppings. Deliveries were made with horse-drawn carts, and there would be horse droppings left behind on the roads. Sometimes a frozen lump of horse dung was just the right size and hard enough to last for a short game before a hard blow would shatter it into flying bits. Nobody ever had to look very long to find another lump to use for a puck.

"There were always horse droppings to use for pucks," Kwong said with a chuckle.

Skates were another matter: equipment that just couldn't be made at home. Borrowing skates from friends worked pretty well for a while. Larry begged his mother for skates of his own. It was hard to justify the expense, when she was a widow raising her many children, but he persisted. He wanted to join the hockey team, and to do that, he would need skates.

Larry made a promise to his mother — that if she could buy him skates he would grow up to become a real hockey player, and then he would be able to buy her a house. With encouragement from the older sons Jack and Jimmy, she agreed that skates were a good idea. The skates she bought for Larry were bigger than his feet, so that he could wear them for a couple of years.

In cold weather, icy roads would be used for play by boys and girls, slipping and sliding in their shoes and boots and sometimes in skates. When Coldstream Avenue froze over, Larry could skate through the Chinatown section of Vernon, instead of just on frozen ponds. There wasn't much vehicle traffic to worry about in the 1920s and 30s: just a few trucks, fewer cars, and some horse-drawn wagons.

Living in Chinatown

There was a Chinatown even in a place as small as Vernon in the 1890s when Eng Kwong arrived, not only because immigrants preferred to live near each other, but because of racist attitudes among Canadians of European origin. The government of British Columbia passed discriminatory legislation against immigrants from Asia and put pressure on the federal government to do likewise. The British Columbia legislature, during its first sessions, passed laws including the Qualifications of Voters Act in 1872, which disenfranchised both First Nations and Chinese people, even those who had become property-owners and taxpayers under the laws of the former Crown

Colony. This was no accident. As one Member of the Legislature said, "Otherwise, we might, after next election, see an Indian occupying the Speaker's chair, or have a Chinese majority in the house."

The year of Larry's birth, 1923, was the year the Chinese Head Tax was finally repealed. But the Canadian government replaced this law with the Chinese Exclusion Act, which for the next twenty-five years barred Chinese persons from entering the country. Any Chinese person who left Canada was not allowed to return.

The Kwong family was lucky they already owned their store and their home above it, because the new legislation made it very difficult for Chinese-Canadians to buy property. In western Canada, discrimination against persons from China or India included prohibitions in some cities against selling a house or business to "Asians." As late as 1986 and 2010, the legal deeds for properties in some parts of Vancouver, BC still included an old clause prohibiting the sale of this property to Asians, because many homeowners never bothered to pay the legal costs to delete that clause. It was not until 1988 the Government of Canada passed the Multicultural Act, which was meant to "ensure that all individuals would receive equal treatment and equal protection under the law, while respecting and valuing their diversity."

In Vernon, the small Chinese population was a minority but an active part of the community, and in many ways close. The Chinese Nationalist League had annual celebrations, and for their sixth gathering in 1925, there were fifty members lined up for a commemorative photograph.

Most of Larry's boyhood experiences were not unusual for any boy in western Canada, and he was not the only boy growing up in Vernon's Chinatown. He was already facing challenges as a young athlete.

Chapter 3: On the Hydrophones

As a boy, Larry Kwong played as an amateur on the Vernon team that won the BC Midget and Juvenile Championships. Even before his feet grew to fit his skates, he showed real promise as a player. It wasn't long before he led his team in scoring goals and assists. His older brothers were proud of him, and they or some of his sisters would come to watch his team play. But his mother was not sure hockey was a smart idea.

"She didn't think too much of hockey. She came to see me play one game. She thought it was too rough, and she wouldn't see another game," he later told Chad Soon for his article "The Longest Shot." "She said, 'Why do you want to play hockey?' I said, 'Because I can earn some money,' and I said, 'I will build you a house with my hockey money.'"

Years later, Larry's daughter, proud of her father's achievement, remembered what she was told of her grandmother's opinion of hockey. "She told my father, 'You should be working and earning money, instead of playing hockey.' But he told her, "You'll see. One day I'll make enough money to build you a house.' And he did."

Hockey Costs

"The average cost for having a child in hockey was $2,898 in 2011-12," reported Allan Maki for the *Globe and Mail*, quoting a study commissioned by Hockey Canada. The cost for the Kwong family in 1936 to have their youngest son play his first season of hockey on a newly-organized official BC minor league team was far less than $2,898. But it was a much larger percentage of their 1936 family income than $3,000 was to an average Canadian family in 2012.

During the Depression, many families in Western Canada were barely able to make a living. In many of the towns and small cities in Canada, most parents were unable to pay for all of their children to receive a high school education or training in a trade or profession. Paying school fees and buying books and paper was a financial burden on a family. It was common for children to wear clothing and shoes handed down from older brothers and sisters, and in some families siblings took turns wearing a warm coat or boots in winter. Of course, hockey jerseys and equipment were second-hand or hand-me-downs as well.

What Were The Odds?

Just playing hockey is no guarantee of growing up to become a professional player. Roy MacGregor wrote for the Toronto *Globe and Mail* in 2013 about "the much less than one-percent chance that any child signing up new this fall has of one day turning this child's play into a life." In the early 1930s, there were six teams in the National Hockey League, with some fourteen players each. That made a total of about 84 players in the league. Each of those teams kept a farm team in the senior leagues. In all of North America's senior hockey leagues, there were only a few hundred professional and semi-professional players hard at work and play, when thirteen-year-old Larry joined his first recreational team.

Minor Hockey Success

It was a grand thing, to play hockey with other boys. Larry made friends there, one of whom was young Don Saunders. With Don playing in goal and Larry as a forward, they were part of an active and effective team: the Vernon Hydrophones.

For Canadian boys growing up in a time before cable television and video games, "our real life was on the skating-rink," wrote Roch Carrier in his timeless book *The Hockey Sweater*. "Real battles were won on the skating-rink. Real strength appeared on the skating-rink. The real leaders showed themselves on the skating-rink." Carrier also remembered that in his youth "...school was also a quiet place where we could prepare for the next hockey game, lay out our next strategies."

Even as a minor league player, Larry made good impressions on his teammates. George Dobie played as a winger on the Hydrophones from 1939 to 1941. A lifelong friend of Larry's, Dobie later became a longtime reporter for the *Vancouver Sun* newspaper. When talking with journalist Chad Soon for an article reprinted on the Society of North American Historians & Researchers SONAHR World Sports History website, Dobie remembered Larry lining up with him as right and left wing. Together they led the team to the BC Midget Championship in 1939.

In Game 1 of the 1939 BC Midget Final in Vernon, over 1000 paying customers in a town of some 5000 people watched Larry Kwong score four unassisted goals in the first period. By the end of the game, Larry had five goals and two assists in the Hydrophone's 12-7 victory over Nelson. By all accounts, it was a barn-burner of a game. In Game 2, won by Vernon 16-4, Larry notched a hat trick plus two assists. He led his team for scoring in the two-game series with a total of twelve points.

In 1940, the Hydrophones lost in the final — the only game they lost that season. The Hydrophones took the 1941 BC Juvenile title in a two-game series. That year the first string forwards were George Dobie, Les Smith, and Larry Kwong, and in Game 1 of the finals they scored all six goals for Vernon to win 6-2. For Game 2, Larry scored half of his team's eight goals, and Don Saunders in goal let only one shot past him.

"Exceptional around the net," said Dobie of his teammate. "He could put it [the puck] up in that top corner better than they do now in the NHL. His hands were quick. Good stick-handler. His skating was perfect. They couldn't touch him. He was too quick."

A team photo from about 1939 shows young Larry Kwong on the Vernon Hydrophones.

Tournament Travel

Success as a team meant that the Hydrophones had tournament games to play in other cities. The team did not rent a bus for these trips, because at that time there simply wasn't money to be raised among the families or in the community for that kind of expense. For travel, the young players would crowd into as few cars or trucks as possible — something that would horrify parents in the 21st century, who are used to local car-pooling on city streets in minivans with a seat belt for each passenger.

In the winter of 1940, the Hydrophones travelled by car for a hockey game in Nelson, BC. Poor road conditions meant the cars carrying the players had to take the best roads available through mountain passes to the Kootenay region of BC. That meant taking roads that would cross the border into the United States, and cross again back into Canada. And that border was a barrier for sixteen-year-old Larry Kwong.

"I hit the border and the American customs would not let me go through—because I was Chinese," Kwong later told journalist Kenda D. Gee. Having his birth certificate showing that he was Canadian by birth was still not enough to allow him to leave Canada. The Chinese Exclusion Act did not allow Chinese or Chinese-Canadians to leave the country; they were allied aliens, not citizens. It would have taken a special form from the federal government Department of Immigration, a C.I. 9, to permit him to leave Canada and return.

"So, I had to get out of the car, take a train — by myself — and stayed on the Canadian side of the border. Then, I met the rest of the team, at the other point in Canada." Riding the Kettle Valley Railroad by himself was an experience many boys might have welcomed, though not for this reason. "I did that two times when I was playing juvenile hockey," Kwong added.

Tennis Match

Years later when they were grown with families of their own, Larry's sister Betty would tell the story of her brother playing tennis in Vernon. His summer job was being a ball-boy at the community centre tennis courts — in the 1930s, that was an age-appropriate job for a young boy wanting to help his family make ends meet. Tennis became his summer sport. Since he was at the community tennis courts a lot, he picked up a number of games playing with whoever was around at the end of the day. Soon he was entering tournaments.

Larry wasn't even ten when he won a tennis tournament at the community centre and qualified to play at the finals across town at the Vernon Country Club. As Betty well remembered, the VCC had to bend its own rules to let a Chinese-Canadian person play at their club. No big fuss was made at the time, but the Chinese community took note that for the first time the Vernon Country Club allowed a person of colour to play. In 1941, Larry won under-18 boys title at the BC Interior Tennis Championships in Kamloops. He beat Maurice Bailargeon to win the Stone Trophy, and took the doubles and mixed doubles titles as well. From there, Larry went on to the provincial championships in Vancouver.

It wasn't only when travelling to the eastern BC towns for hockey tournaments that young Larry was unable to drive with his team mates on highways crossing the American border. In 1941 there were few paved highways between the Okanagan valley and Vancouver. When roads washed out in bad weather, travellers would have to drive other routes through Washington state to the coast, or ride a train. "When I came down to Vancouver to play in a junior tennis tournament — it was the same thing," Kwong told journalist Kenda Gee. "I had to get off and take a train by myself."

Looking to the Future

As a Canadian of Chinese descent, Kwong's background came to affect his life, his work, and his hockey experiences in ways that were not a factor for Maurice Richard in Quebec or Howie Meeker in Ontario before those men joined the NHL. For example, long before he finished his teens, young Larry realized he could not plan to earn a living in Vernon. Two of his brothers ran the family store, with Jim eventually concentrating more on trucking farm produce and Jack going to Calgary to work in another Chinese grocery. Two other brothers had gone to Vancouver to try their luck working for other Chinese businesses. Many of his older sisters, too, had to take whatever jobs they could find with Chinese stores in the nearby small cities of Vernon, Kamloops, and Ashcroft. Careers as professionals were not open to Chinese-Canadians because of the Exclusion Act of 1923.

Being a good student in school was helpful for some of his siblings. His youngest sister Ina looked forward to working in an office some day, but young Larry felt he was a poor student. He was good in track and field, but he wasn't proud of his grades in other studies. A career as a hockey player looked like his best option.

Chapter 4: A Smoke Eater

THERE WEREN'T MANY alternatives to succeeding at hockey for a young man in the Okanagan valley, if the law kept him from working for any of the businesses in Vernon and the other towns. In 1940 it was illegal for a Chinese-Canadian to enter a profession, and it was legal for business owners to discriminate against hiring people of Chinese descent. Larry Kwong wasn't the only young man affected. Of the five hundred or more Chinese people living nearby in the Okanagan valley, nearly all of them were farmers and farm labourers. Few were shopkeepers or cooks.

The Kwong siblings worked hard to earn their living. To bring produce from the farms, his brother Jim drove a truck. In good years, he was able to hire a few drivers — even some white men, Larry noticed, if they were good workers, an irony not lost on Larry. His sisters were kept busy in the family store, which was now listed on page 397 in the 1938 business directory for BC and the Yukon as selling crockery, fancy goods and groceries. Even with experience keeping records for their business, they couldn't get jobs working for other local businesses as clerks. As the youngest son, Larry could see the hard work his brothers did and the long hours his sisters spent in the store. He knew there wasn't much other work available for him near Vernon but being a physical labourer on someone else's farm for low wages.

There was some work as a logger cutting trees. Logging was even harder physical labour than farming and perhaps the most dangerous work available in North America. Lumber mills had better working conditions. There were mines operating locally, as well. In his teenage years, Larry applied for work at many companies, but each time he was told "The owners won't let us hire Chinese workers." To his family, Larry would say that the companies didn't need anyone, or they weren't hiring anyone. He couldn't bear to tell them why he wasn't hired. He was raised to work hard, and not to complain.

For work on a fishing boat or cannery, he would have to go as far as Vancouver or the sea coast and try his luck. He couldn't join the Armed Forces, an option for work that was available to most young white Canadian men. As an allied alien Larry wasn't even eligible to be drafted though it was wartime.

So he tried his best to become a hockey player. And he made it to one of the best teams in the Alberta-BC Senior Hockey League and in the world — the Trail Smoke Eaters. At the small city of Trail in the Kootenay region of BC, there was both an indoor rink in the Fruit Fair Building, and a champion hockey team.

A photo of the Smoke Eaters from 1941 shows Larry Kwong among his teammates.

Local Sports Heroes

It can be hard for people with modern access to cable television and the Internet to realize just how much interest there was in the 1930s and 40s for local sports. Local games were not just ways for growing boys to have fun, they were a vital part of a community, providing recreation, entertainment for many people, and employment for young men. Hockey games in particular were covered in local newspapers by reporters who passed the news on to major newspapers and CBC radio. Sometimes national papers would carry the news about a particularly good game far from Toronto or Montreal, or about which team won the championship in a regional senior league.

In towns and small cities throughout BC and Alberta, particularly mining communities, there was an intense rivalry among hockey teams that began at the turn of the century. By 1901, the Smoke Eaters were already a team celebrated in newspapers. Their name was a reference to the pall of smoke which hung over Trail from the Cominco smelter. The smelter had been operating since 1895, smelting copper and gold at first, quickly switching to lead and zinc, and later sulphur as well. Nobody liked breathing the sooty emissions, but some people said that it smelled like money and progress. Others claimed that breathing the smoke of mills and smelters would kill germs that made people sick. The smoky emissions were toxic with lead and sulphur dioxide.

As recreational hockey leagues became formally organized in the southern parts of British Columbia, teams in the Okanagan and Kootenay regions were able to pick and choose the best players. These teams were not considered professional, as they didn't pay their players a salary, but found them good jobs in the mines and smelters. Working for a mining company brought these men much better wages than anything they could earn as clerks or farm workers. During the Depression, it was very difficult for anyone to find work of any kind. Later, during the war years, mining workers were providing essential services, and so were not drafted into the Armed Forces.

By winning the 1938 Allan Cup for the national senior hockey championship, the Smoke Eaters earned the right to represent

Canada in international play. In December 1938, the Smoke Eaters travelled to Europe, representing Canada in the 1939 World Hockey Championship. They were undefeated against teams which had previously competed in the Olympics, including the Soviet national team. After winning the championship, they played an exhausting tour of exhibition games in which they were undefeated, mostly on outdoor rinks throughout Europe, including England and Scotland. Their final exhibition game was in Switzerland before a crowd of nineteen thousand — an exciting experience for a team from a town that didn't have even seven thousand citizens fifty years later in 1990. When Larry Kwong came to play for the Smoke Eaters in 1941, he knew he was now a real hockey player, playing for a champion team.

In his Smoke Eaters jersey, Larry Kwong looks like the star forward he became for the team.

Why Call Him Clipper?

On the ice, Larry Kwong picked up a nickname among sports

journalists. They called him The China Clipper. The first use of this nickname was in newspapers in Vernon in 1940. In Merritt, BC the newspaper even ran an ad declaring: "At the Merritt Arena — Don't fail to see Lawrence Kwong, of the Hydrophones (named by hockey fans as the China Clipper) ." The nickname was picked up by a Calgary broadcaster, when the West Kootenay Hockey League extended itself to include two teams from southern Alberta. The broadcaster called games for both hockey and football; later he used the same nickname for Normie Kwong, who in 1948 became the first player of Chinese descent in the Canadian Football League.

This nickname was a cheerful and contemporary reference to Kwong's speed on the ice and his ability to deliver the puck. The clippers were large sailing ships that crossed the Atlantic and Pacific Oceans. Rigged with three masts and square sails, some of the clipper ships like *Cutty Sark* and *Thermopylae* were famous in their day. These ships were reliable transport for goods and passengers for many decades in the 1800s. Kwong's father emigrated from southern China to Canada on a clipper. Passage could take two months and it was no pleasure cruise. But it was far more prompt and reliable than "a slow boat to China" — a slow cargo vessel with a blocky shape and fewer sails than a slender clipper, that could take many months to deliver parcels and mail across the Pacific.

When airplanes began making regular trips across the ocean, it's no surprise that one airline named their planes for clippers rather than slow barges. The actual *China Clipper* was a Pan American Airways plane that made the first commercial trans-Pacific air service between San Francisco and Manila. On its first flight in November 1935, the four-engine seaplane became a worldwide sensation taking only seven days to deliver one hundred and ten thousand pieces of mail across the Pacific Ocean. The next summer, Warner Brothers studio released a film called *China Clipper*, co-starring a young Humphrey Bogart. *China Clipper* delivered air mail and passengers until 1945, along with sister planes *Hawaii Clipper* and *Philippine Clipper*.

Photos from Kwong's time playing for the Smoke Eaters in 1941 and 42 show him to be a trim, muscular young man with smooth dark hair and clear skin. Calling him The China Clipper was a compliment, likening him to movie star Humphrey Bogart and to the modern service of air mail.

A Smoke Eaters team photo shows Larry Kwong playing center forward, with his two wingmen.

A Chinese Player

All team members of the Trail Smoke Eaters had high-paying jobs at the local smelter for Cominco. But there was no job there for Larry when he joined the team. He tried to wait patiently, but there was no explanation. Months later, one of the directors admitted to him privately that it was a Cominco policy — no Chinese persons were allowed to work at the smelter.

It was an emotional blow to be treated differently from the rest of the team, but Larry had been raised by his family not to be outspoken about such discrimination. To be seen and not heard was the way he had been taught. He had learned from his brothers to work hard and well, and not to complain. "It leaves a mark on you," Kwong later said to journalist David Davis. "You feel that you're not one of the boys."

Instead, the team managed to find him a job as a bellhop in the Crown Point Hotel in Trail. It didn't pay nearly as much as the factory work at the smelter, but Larry was a young man who knew how to work. He appreciated that the hotel owner Mr. Kerr gave him the chance, and never forgot that someone cared to give him this job.

Even so, working there barely paid for his room. In 1941, bellhops could expect no tips except on the rare times a travelling salesman would come to town. "They'd always have heavy cases to carry to their rooms, full of samples," Kwong remembered. "And sometimes, they would tip a little." While working at the hotel, he would hear Mr. Kerr speaking French, and resolved that someday he should learn French too. It seemed something that a sophisticated businessman would do.

The Crown Point Hotel had a Chinese cook who was sympathetic to the young man with no wages left to buy food. The cook would simply call him in to the kitchen and give him a good hot meal, noodles and vegetables like he was used to from home. He deserved a good meal, said the cook, and he was working hard. After a few months the team quietly began to make up some of the difference in wages between a bellhop and the smelter jobs. Eventually the team provided for Kwong by arranging for his meals with a good Chinese family who ran a restaurant in Trail. These considerations showed that he had come to be respected by his team manager, even if he was not treated the same as the other players because of societal standards.

At the end of the 1941-42 season, Senior Hockey was suspended in the West Kootenay region because of the number of men called for military service. It was time for Kwong to look for another team and another job. Enlisting in the Armed Forces was not an option open to him. But other possibilities became available to him.

Reporter Hank Viney brought Kwong to the attention of the manager for the Cleveland Barons, a minor professional team playing for the American Hockey league. The team expressed interest in Kwong, but he wasn't able to go to the United States. He looked for a better offer, or a Canadian team to join. And there were times when young Larry Kwong dreamed that someday he might, just might, be able to go anywhere.

Chapter 5: Service in War Years

THE DREAM YOUNG Larry Kwong shared with many players in the senior leagues came true. Coaches for the Chicago Black Hawks sent Kwong an invitation to attend their training camp in 1942. This was the big break he had been waiting for — he had been scouted for a team in the National Hockey League.

With excitement, Kwong applied to the Canadian Immigration department for documents, such as a C.I. 9 certificate, that would give him permission to leave the country to attend training camp. He didn't want to face any problems at the American border, as he had in his teens when he was going to hockey and tennis tournaments. But the Canadian government turned down his application. And under the Exclusion Act, if he ever left the country, he would not be allowed to return. As much as Kwong wanted to play in the world's top hockey league, he didn't want it more than the ability to return to his family and home. With regret, Kwong had to turn down the offer from the Black Hawks team manager. He would have to look for other opportunities within Canada.

On the Coast

When opportunity knocked, Kwong was ready to answer the

call. After the 1941-42 season with the Smoke Eaters, Kwong had a good offer from the Nanaimo Clippers. Many of their team's players worked on the docks, the team managers told him, and at a good rate of pay. He moved to Nanaimo, BC, on Vancouver Island and played there for the Clippers for the 1942-43 season in the Pacific Coast Hockey League.

"I was a labourer," Kwong later told journalist Tom Hawthorne in an interview. "It was a really tough job because it was cold as heck by the ocean. It was really, really cold. You freeze yourself all day and then you had to play hockey all night." Growing up in the Okanagan valley, Kwong had become used to winter being dry and cold. It was a big shock to his system to work on the docks in rainy weather. Dock workers could get soaked to the skin for hours in temperatures near freezing. He lost more heat in wet clothes than he ever had playing hockey on rinks and ponds.

Playing hard in Nanaimo brought Kwong the attention of NHL agents for the Boston Bruins. He even had an offer to join their farm team. Most senior league hockey players could only dream of this kind of good news, and now it had happened again to him! Twice now he had been scouted by an NHL team, and chosen as one of the best prospects.

But Kwong's birth certificate and identification papers were still not enough for him to leave the country to attend training camp and play hockey. Kwong wrote again to the federal government to ask for special permission to go to the United States. This time, his request was refused because he was a man of the right age to be conscripted into the army. For years, he kept the telegram with that official reply among the records of his hockey career. The fact that there was a law keeping Canadian-born allied aliens of Chinese descent from being drafted did not matter; Kwong was not able to go to Boston and accept the offer from the Bruins.

The war continued, and Kwong continued to play hockey and work at the jobs that were available. But working at the docks was hard physical labour, as hard as the farm labour Kwong had left behind in the Okanagan valley. Doing hard work outdoors in the rain was not a fun way to spend the winter, especially for someone from the Okanagan's drier climate. And after a hard day's work, it was difficult to play hard on the ice. Even so, he made a good impression on the managers of another team in the Pacific Coast Hockey League — Vancouver's St Regis hockey team. When they made him an offer, Kwong moved to Vancouver in 1943.

Once in Vancouver, Kwong had a good place to stay, at the St Regis Hotel. Like most players in the Senior Leagues, he needed a job to pay his bills. In Vancouver, his work was in a coffee shop down the street from the St Regis Hotel. This work kept him warmer, and didn't affect how he played hockey at night. But partway through the 1943-44 season, everything changed.

The first change came when left winger David 'Sweeney' Schriner joined the Vancouver St Regis team. Schriner's career was in a changing state: he had left the NHL to play for a Canadian military team in the Alberta Garrison League. At the end of that league's season, Schriner signed on with St Regis as the team prepared for the playoffs. He played three games before an opposing team complained that Schriner was an NHL player and therefore a professional. The protest resulted in the entire St Regis team being suspended by the Canadian Amateur Hockey Association (CAHA). In vain, Schriner appealed, citing the prior CAHA rule that automatically restored the amateur status of all active military personnel. But an officer in the Naval reserve isn't the same as a soldier on active duty. The appeal did not succeed.

The appeal didn't make much difference for Kwong, as St Regis was eliminated in the playoffs. What made more difference for Kwong was the second big change which came at that time: official notice from the government that he had been drafted for military service. As well, though he didn't know it then, the young center forward had come to the attention of Schriner, who spread the word about the China Clipper to his contacts in the Central Garrison League.

War Service

In 1944, the government began drafting Chinese-Canadians to serve in special operations in the Asia-Pacific theatres. Among the first of these men to be conscripted was Larry Kwong. He was sent for basic training in Red Deer, Alberta.

The idea behind selecting men of Chinese descent to serve in the Armed Forces was that some of them would be safer overseas in special operations than men of European descent because they might be able to 'blend in' with people of a similar racial background. But it soon became clear that Kwong was something even rarer than a Chinese-Canadian soldier: he was a terrific hockey player.

"Some of those boys went overseas and got killed," Kwong told journalist Chad Soon for an article reprinted on SONAHR World Sports History website. He lost many friends that way. "Luckily for me, they kept me to play hockey to entertain the troops." Some of those Chinese-Canadians who served died overseas, while others returned to their hometowns as veterans decorated with military honours, able to make changes to improve racial equality in schools, recreation, and work.

War service provided another big break for Kwong, in the form of playing hockey in the Central Garrison League. Years later, when journalist Tom Hawthorne asked a retired Larry Kwong what he did during the war, Kwong replied that he "fought the battle of Wetaskiwin" — where the soldiers shot pucks instead of bullets. It's probable that teams in the Central Garrison League learned about Larry Kwong from 'Sweeney' Schriner, but Kwong's reputation in the newspaper may have been enough to turn heads in the League.

He played first for the Red Deer Wheelers in the Central Garrison league, with goalie 'Sugar Jim' Henry and Mac Colville, men who were stars for the New York Rangers. Later on in his service, Kwong played on the Wetaskiwin Army team. He caught the attention of Charlie Rayner, goalie for Royal Canadian Navy teams based out of Victoria, BC. The Colville brothers playing for the Ottawa Commandos faced off against Kwong and the Army, with Neil Colville at centre and Mac Colville at right wing. When the Colvilles returned from their military service to play as defencemen for the New York Rangers, they and Rayner and Henry brought stories of the little forward who could turn fast as a doodlebug on skates. Word about Kwong spread to the Rangers coaches, and to the head coach of their farm team, the New York Rovers.

As the war ended, so did his military service. While Kwong returned to Trail in 1945 and played another season for the Smoke

Eaters, coaches for the New York Rangers made their own plans. The Smoke Eaters became the BC Champions for the 1945-46 season, with Larry Kwong in the forward line. With teammate Mike Buckna, Kwong was top scorer in the playoffs for the Smoke Eaters. He scored the goal that won the Savage Cup.

After the season ended, Kwong had an offer from a team in the Pacific Coast Amateur League on April 30. On August 6, Kwong received another offer, this time from the Kimberley Dynamiters in the newly-formed Western International Hockey League. He held out as long as he could, and then a telegram came from Lester Patrick. The New York Rangers made him an offer, the third offer he had received from an NHL team. This time he was able to accept. Military service had brought Kwong and other Chinese-Canadian servicemen the rights of full citizens.

The Rangers brought Kwong to Winnipeg for their annual hockey school. It was there that manager Frank Boucher offered him a contract for their farm team, the New York Rovers, in the Eastern Hockey League (EHL), under Rovers head coach Fred Metcalfe.

The Immigration Department Connection

Immigration policy is neither a sidebar to Larry Kwong's story nor a distraction from his hockey career. It is an issue intimately tied to his hockey history. The reason began long before Kwong was born, and it began with a prominent civil servant in Canada's Immigration department, Frederick Wellington Taylor. Ontario-born 'Cyclone' Taylor was one of hockey's first star players. He was also one of the first to be paid as a professional player. In 1907, Fred Taylor began employment in the Department of the Interior's Immigration Branch, a job he received as encouragement to play for the Ottawa Senators team. Taylor moved from Ottawa to Vancouver and was playing hockey there and working in Immigration at the time Larry Kwong's mother arrived in Canada. By 1914, Taylor was the number 3 immigration official in Vancouver during the infamous events surrounding the steamship *Komagata Maru*. In the short seasons played at that time, Taylor would match his government salary in only twenty games.

When Larry Kwong was a child in the 1930s, Taylor was

Commissioner of Immigration for BC and Yukon. Though retired as a hockey player, Cyclone Taylor was president of the Pacific Coast Hockey League from 1936 to 1940. When Kwong was writing for permission to leave the country, the top immigration official was Taylor. As Commissioner, Taylor was ultimately responsible for Larry Kwong being unable to take either of his first two offers from NHL teams. Taylor was also coaching the Vancouver St Regis team while Kwong played centre forward for them in 1943.

A 1943 article in the Vancouver Province newspaper noted that Taylor thought highly of Kwong and suggested that Lester Patrick should acquire him for the Rangers. When Kwong's time playing for St Regis came to an abrupt end at his enlistment in the armed forces, he didn't end up in training for Special Forces, to do guerrilla fighting and demolition in southeast Asia. Was it the influence of Taylor or Patrick that put young soldier Kwong in the Garrison League instead of sending him into combat? It was certainly Taylor's influence that led to the Rangers considering Kwong as a possible player.

Turns on a Dime

There are several mentions in newspapers during the 1940s of Larry Kwong, and in some he's called a doodlebug. Doodlebug is not just a colloquialism, and it's not only a name for wind-up metal toys that spin around, named for flying beetles with buzzing wings. In 1944, doodlebug was a nickname for the German V-1 rockets used to bomb London and southern England. People told stories of hearing the rockets pass overhead, unexpectedly fast with a buzzing engine sound. Sometimes the V-1 rockets were seen to change direction, or go silent and fall suddenly, with powerful explosions in devastating attacks. Over 9,500 of these buzz bombs fell on southern England in 1944.

When Larry Kwong was described by players and journalists as a doodlebug on skates, this was a statement of admiration for his speed and power. It meant he was fast enough to hurtle past opposing players. Like these steered rockets, Kwong could turn on a dime and give you nine cents change. His knees took the stress and turned him smoothly in unexpected directions. The sound of his skates on ice was likened to a powerful war engine, by people who had heard V-1 rockets in flight. While the word doodlebug is still used these days for a little wind-up toy, someone wanting to give a hockey player this epithet might call him a buzz bomb, or a cruise missile.

A Professional Appearance

Now Kwong was headed for New York City! His family shared the news with excitement, read his acceptance letter together, and helped him prepare. A home haircut made him neat and presentable. His skates were sharpened and ready.

There was only one problem remaining. The acceptance letter, which came by telegraph, said all hockey players when travelling must wear a tie and suit to present a professional image. Larry didn't own a suit. That wasn't unusual in 1946, among young working men or lower-income families. But the family pulled together and obtained him a suit. His mother tidied an old suit jacket that belonged to his older brother, and Larry got a new pair of gray flannel trousers. He shined his shoes. With a tie fastened by his brother, and a neatly-brushed hat, Larry had the professional image he needed. He boarded the train, looking the part of the fine young professional hockey player that he was.

"At that time, I hadn't learned how to tie a necktie," Kwong confessed later in conversation. "At night, I slipped the tie over my head and kept it tied so it would be ready to wear the next day."

At age 23, Larry Kwong was about to live his dream of playing for an NHL team. And now, because of his service in the Armed Forces, he was as able as any other Canadian citizen to leave Canada, visit other countries, and return. He was headed for Lake Placid for training camp, and on to play in New York City.

Chapter 6: King Kwong in New York

IN 1946 KWONG was picked up by an NHL team, the New York Rangers, for their farm team. That year Larry was one of seventy players attending the Rangers' annual amateur hockey school in Winnipeg, Manitoba. He went on for training at Lake Placid, New York, and then to New York City. Manager Frank Boucher signed Larry Kwong on at age twenty-three, a rookie and former serviceman among many such players.

Coaches

The manager and head coach for the New York Rangers was himself Canadian: Frank Boucher was born in Ottawa in 1901, andhad been an NHL player, along with three of his older brothers. He'd been awarded the Lady Byng Memorial Trophy for sportsmanlike conduct seven times, , which is given to the player who exhibits the best type of sportsmanship and gentlemanly conduct combined with a high standard of playing ability. Statistics are compared, to see who combines the highest score with the lowest number of penalty minutes, but there is a subjective element as well to the selection. When the league retired the original silver trophy in 1936, it was given to Boucher to keep. This was a man who understood fair play in sports. After fourteen seasons in the NHL, Boucher turned to coaching for the Rangers.

The Rovers' head coach, Fred Metcalfe, was considered one of the best coaches in the senior leagues. He had a Canadian past of his own when he turned to coaching after ten years as a player; he coached two seasons for the Lethbridge Maple Leafs in the Alberta Senior Hockey League from 1938 to 1940. It's possible that during his time in Lethbridge, Metcalfe might have heard of young Larry Kwong who was then playing for the Vernon Hydrophones. In the 1940-41 season, Metcalfe led the Regina Rangers to win the Allan Cup in the Saskatchewan Senior Hockey League, before becoming the head coach for the New York Rovers in the Eastern Hockey League (EHL).

Like Kwong, Metcalfe had done military service during WWII. In February 1942, Metcalfe enlisted in the U.S. Army, fighting with the 77th Artillery. The Rovers had different coaches assisting until the 1945-46 season when Metcalfe returned. As the Milwaukee Journal reported, with a new promotion program in the American Hockey League, Metcalfe was handed "the task of trying to develop new talent where hockey talent never has been found before."

Contract Negotiations

Negotiating his contract with the 'Blueshirts' of the NHL had Kwong feeling very much like a small-town boy out of place in the big city. There were four big gentlemen in the room when he came to that meeting, all of them with big cigars and their feet up on the table. He had to manage his own contract talks with Muzz Patrick, Lynn Patrick, Lester Patrick, and Phil Watson. It's no surprise that players in the NHL and on the farm teams were paid modestly at that time. With no union and no agents to speak for them, players were unable to negotiate their contracts from a position of confidence and strength.

It's probable that rather than a lower wage, Kwong was paid more than other players starting out. It was not common to discuss one's wages at that time, but he believed the average hockey player was being paid US$5,000 a season. A few NHL players have confirmed this wage; the most that Wally Stanowski earned in a season, according to sports columnist Damien Cox, was $5,000 playing for the Toronto Maple Leafs between 1939 and 1948. As well, journalist Garth Woolsey reported: "As a rookie with the Red Wings in 1946-47, (Gordie) Howe recalled his salary was $5,000." "I was getting $6,000, which was good money for senior hockey in those days," he told journalist Kendra Gee in a 1994 interview. "I got a little bit more — at least, I think I got a little bit more — because I was Chinese, and they thought that I was more of a drawing [card]."

There was a $100 signing bonus offered, but Kwong didn't take it, and so he was later free to sign with other teams. This was a wise move. While taking the signing bonus would have got him a hundred dollars right away, it would have taken away his option to play for another team. He wanted to keep his options open.

Playing on a Farm Team

For two seasons in the Eastern Hockey League (EHL) and Quebec Senior Hockey League (QSHL), Larry Kwong played for the Rovers, a farm team for the Rangers. One of the main differences between the Rangers and the Rovers was noted in the Brooklyn Daily Eagle: "Larry (King) Kwong, youthful Chinese Canadian, has been sent to the Rovers by the Hockey Rangers which means he will be seen at the [Madison Square] Garden Sunday afternoons instead of Sunday evenings."

He was far from the only Canuck on the team. At least twenty-two of the thirty players in the 1946-47 season were Canadian-born. The next year, there were fifty-five Rovers, more than half of them Canadian.

During that first season he wore number 6, and later he usually wore number 12. Kwong played centre forward, with Hub Anslow at left wing, and Nick Mickoski on right wing. Among his teammates were Jean-Paul Denis and Vic Corbin at right wing, and Fred Shero on defense. It was 'Freddy the Fog' who in 1945 with Coach Metcalfe devised the 'box formation' to use while killing penalties. Shero was a roommate for Kwong on some of the away games.

A farm team is a team in a senior hockey league or a minor professional league, owned and operated by an NHL team. Most of a team's choices for new players come from their farm team. When a team player is unable to play, the coach will bring up a few players from the farm team to dress for a game and be ready as replacements. These replacement players were an especially important support for NHL teams in the 1940s and 1950s when there were only six teams in the league. Often a team had as few as a dozen official players, instead of three full shifts. The farm teams played in many of the same arenas and travelled for away games just as the NHL teams.

Looking back at publicity efforts for the Rangers, it seems there might have been some element of publicity in the hiring of a Chinese player for their farm team in an all-white hockey league. The New York Rangers had already hired a Chinese hypnotist, and a Chinese magician. But no one called Larry Kwong a novelty act. Anyone's concern that hiring a Chinese player might be a publicity stunt disappeared when he began playing. During his first game for the Rovers, he scored a goal against the Boston Olympics.

"I was impressed during virtually every game with Kwong's speed, smarts and teamsmanship," was the opinion of Stan Fischler, a hockey writer and broadcaster for decades. "In a way he reminded me of Hall of Famer Yvan Cournoyer, the Montreal Canadiens forward nicknamed 'Roadrunner.'" On the ice, Kwong was a fast and effective player, and it was obvious to all observers he was one of the best. Coach Metcalfe told him once "he wished he had had a shot like mine," Kwong later told journalist David Davis. "He thought I had one of the fastest releases."

Kwong's status as a drawing-card might explain why the Rangers management kept him for their farm team in New York, rather than assigning him to their New Haven farm team in the American Hockey League. "In those halcyon post-war days," wrote hockey historian Stan Fischler, "the Rovers were almost as popular in Gotham as the Rangers and crowds of more than twelve thousand to fifteen thousand were not uncommon. In fact, on one Sunday, the Rovers actually drew more fans than the parent Rangers."

Living a Dream

In fulfillment of his boyhood dreams, Larry Kwong became an experienced, professional hockey player in the finest arenas in North America. Part-way through his first season with the Rovers, they played in Madison Square Gardens on December 28, 1946, against the Valleyfield Braves from Quebec Senior Hockey League. As a boy, he'd listened to radio coverage of hockey games in Madison Square Gardens. The arena he'd heard echoing to the announcers' commentaries and roars from the crowd now echoed around him as his team played. And afterward, the Valleyfield coach Toe Blake sought him out, to meet him personally and offer him a place on their team. It was heady praise from a professional — Hector 'Toe' Blake was both a coach for the senior leagues and an NHL player for the Montreal Canadiens. The previous season, Blake had been awarded the Lady Byng Trophy. Somehow Kwong managed to turn down Blake's offer and still make a good impression.

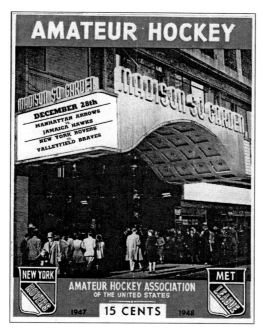

This program shows Madison Square Gardens was the scene for games played by the Rovers as well as NHL games.

The year 1946 was an exciting time to be a professional athlete, and even more, to be an example of racial tolerance. Only a few months earlier, baseball player Jackie Robinson had signed a contract with the Dodgers; the next April he broke the colour barrier in professional baseball. Clearly, New York City was the place to be. Kwong knew of Robinson's place on the New York team during the same time he lived in New York. It's sad to think the two men never met and shared their experiences. Years later, Kwong confided to film-maker Chad Soon that he admired Jackie Robinson very much, but he never had the chance to meet the baseball legend. The life of a professional athlete is very much occupied with a full schedule of practises and games, and Kwong wasn't one to spend a lot of money on recreation like tickets to baseball games.

"Oh, I did spend some money on myself," Kwong admitted later in conversation. But he also arranged for much of his pay to be sent home to his family, for savings and to help support his mother. His brother Jack had moved to Calgary, Alberta and expanded the family grocery into a thriving business. With most of their siblings scattering and some moving to Calgary, this was a time of change for the Kwong family.

Keeping a Promise

It was while playing for the Rovers Kwong was able to keep the promise he'd made as a boy to his mother. It was time for her to retire to a house built for her as he'd promised long ago, paid for with his hockey earnings. It had taken more time than he had hoped, but he met his goal before he was twenty-five years old.

Kwong's older sister Betty was looking after their mother in Calgary, Alberta. At his request, Betty managed the financing for him, meeting with the bank on behalf of her brother who was living in New York. Kwong was pleased Betty arranged to have a house built on the lot next door to their older brother Jack' in Calgary. In 1947 their mother moved to her fine new house, where Betty was able to look after her and her home.

Cultural Hero

The new player for the Rovers became well-known among fans and the media. He was honoured in Chinatown as a cultural hero and role model for youth. In a humbling tribute, during a game on November 17, 1946, Larry Kwong was given the keys to New York City's Chinatown at centre ice by Shavey Lee, the Chamber of Commerce chairman who was known as the unofficial 'Mayor of Chinatown', flanked by two of the China Dolls showgirls. The showgirls Lily Pon and May Dong were all charm and smiles for the blushing hero.

Photographs of this tribute show a striking fact in addition to a small lipstick kiss on his cheek: Kwong in his skates stands no taller than the showgirls in their pretty shoes. Even in his hockey gear, he doesn't bulk much bigger around than the China Dolls. At 5' 6" (165 cm) and 145 pounds (66 kg), he was one of the smallest professional hockey players of the day. Professional players since 2010 tend to be taller and bigger than players in the 1940s. Plenty of players at that time were considered small, like the Rangers forward 'Eager' Edgar Laprade at 5' 8" (175 cm) and 165 lbs (75kg), but few were as small as Kwong. Even Yvan Cournoyer was all of 5' 7" (170 cm) when he joined the NHL in 1963.

[This autographed photo from Kwong's collection shows him receiving the keys to the city, in an on-ice tribute.]

Unnecessary Roughness

All players are not equal on the ice. Big players often find their mass makes them hard for other players to stop or re-direct. Small players might find they are able to change direction and speed far more quickly than the bigger players around them. On the ice, some hockey players are willing to put their bigger size to use when body-checking or fighting. Penalties are meant to keep rough play to a minimum, but to some players a few minutes in a penalty box is a small price to pay after a rough collision or a quick punch. Based on his record which shows few penalty minutes, Kwong was one of the players who didn't find penalties were worth it. You can't score goals while sitting in a penalty box, and he was playing to win games.

"The small fellow with some ability is smashed by the guy with muscle," complained Rangers player Edger Laprade in 1948 when threatening to quit the NHL to return to the Senior Leagues. At 5' 8", Laprade was considered one of the smaller players in the NHL. Later, he was quoted by journalist Tom Hawthorn as saying: "Who can think about the Lady Byng Trophy when there is a stick in your face?"

This trading card was released in 2011 as part of a Canadiana series

Called up to the Rangers

It didn't escape Kwong's notice that several of his Rovers teammates had played a game or two for the Rangers, or even been called onto the team as regulars. But after a year and a half, the Rangers had never yet called on Kwong to play for them.

In his second season with the Rovers, Kwong led the team in scoring with eighty-five points in sixty-five games. As the leading scorer for the team — and the league — he received an award from the team at a brief ceremony during a game. No Rover had scored better in almost a decade. Even so, when injuries sidelined some of their regular players, the Rangers tried four other Rover forwards that season instead of Kwong.

It was not until March 1948, late in the 1947-48 season, that Kwong was called up from the farm team to play for the New York Rangers. On their way to Montreal, the team was going to be short a couple of players who had fallen ill. Their bad luck created an opportunity for Kwong and Ronnie Rowe, another Rover.

Kwong already had a lot on his mind. During a game against Quebec, Coach Metcalfe had a heart attack. He was still in hospital when Kwong learned he was to play in Montreal for the Rangers. As Kwong told journalist Chad Soon years later, it pleased Metcalfe immensely to hear the news. "Larry, they finally brought you up," he said. "You should have been up there a long time ago."

In the Forum

Montreal Forum was the scene where the Rangers played against the Montreal Canadiens on March 13, 1948. When Larry put on the 'Blueshirt' uniform for the Rangers, he was given number 11, though he usually wore 12 for the Rovers. "I was very nervous, because we had lots of publicity on it — being the first Chinese to play in the NHL," Kwong told Chad Soon, decades later, and sighed. "I was very disappointed I didn't get a better chance to prove myself."

In spite of his excitement, Kwong kept calm on the bench as the game began. He found the patience to wait as the first period went by, watching Maurice Richard and Doug Harvey playing for the Canadiens. Kwong knew he wouldn't be facing the Canadiens' 'Punch Line' of Richard, Elmer Lach and Toe Blake, as earlier that season in January Blake had suffered a double fracture of his ankle.

The second period passed, and he hadn't been sent to play. It wasn't until late in the third period Coach Boucher finally called Kwong's name to send him out to take a shift on the ice. Larry was so eager, he didn't even wait to open the gate. He slipped over the boards and onto the ice. Smoothly, he moved down the rink, and passed the puck to a teammate. "All I wanted to do was to play hockey," he said, speaking of that moment to journalist Chad Soon.

Among the promotional photos taken before the game was this image
of Larry Kwong to be sent out on the wire service to sports media.

In less than a minute, the shift was over. All the Rangers players went back to the bench, and another shift took the ice. As the clock ticked away the last moments of the third period, there was 3:37 left to play when 'Rocket' Richard set up Hall of Fame defenseman Ken Rearden, who scored for the Canadiens. Montreal won the game, 3 to 2. The game was over.

Afterwards

Years later in 2013, Kwong would speak of this disappointing game to journalist David Davis, and say: "I didn't get a chance to show what I can do." He was not given a fair shot to prove himself, but at least, after two seasons, he had been allowed to play. Six more years would pass before a man of colour would play in an NHL game, when First Nations player Fred Sasakamoose played for the Chicago Blackhawks in 1954. It was ten years after Kwong's single NHL game that the Boston Bruins would sign player Willie O'Ree, the first black player in the NHL.

After the Rangers game in Montreal, Kwong returned with the team to New York City. The Rangers had another game the very next day, against the Canadiens, and they called on Ronnie Rowe, but they didn't call Kwong to dress for the game. Rowe ended up playing five games that season, as it turned out.

Kwong returned to the Rovers. There was still a week left to play in the season. A few days later, word came that Rovers coach Fred Metcalfe had resigned, due to his heart condition. Things looked bleak for Kwong's future with the Rangers and Rovers, but he had other opportunities to explore.

Chapter 7: The China Clipper Back in Canada

A BETTER OFFER from the Valleyfield Braves, including a higher rate of pay than he had in New York, brought Kwong back to Canada for nine great seasons in the Quebec Senior League. With the loss of the coach who had supported him strongly, Kwong knew he would never be given a fair chance to prove himself on the ice in the NHL. But Fred Metcalfe was not the only coach to recognise his talent.

It was not an easy choice for Kwong, when he decided to leave the New York Rovers and his NHL hopes. A good offer had been made to him in his first season, by Toe Blake as coach for the Valleyfield Braves in the Quebec Senior Hockey League. At that time, Kwong had turned down the offer, and managed to do so without offense.

Now the offer was renewed by the team owner himself, Arthur Vinet. The Braves would not only hire him — they'd put him on the ice, as a forward. And they'd even pay him more than he was earning in New York, plus an additional bonus system. For every point he scored through goals and assists, they'd give him a $5 bonus. With Coach 'Toe' Blake who had just endured an injury that ended his own NHL career as a player, Kwong knew he had advantages of his own as a player. After having to give up his own NHL dreams, a player-coach like Blake would understand Kwong and why he would keep on doing his best.

"I couldn't refuse that offer," Kwong told reporter Hugues Théorêt years later. "At any rate, I had no future in New York."

It wasn't an easy choice to leave an NHL farm team for another team in a senior league, but it was a good choice for both Kwong and his new team. When Blake's ankle healed, he took to the ice as a player-coach, so that between Blake and Kwong, the Valleyfield Braves had two lines of powerful forwards.

Kwong is shown here in Valleyview, with his coach Toe Blake.

Seven Stellar Seasons with the Braves

In Quebec, Kwong played amazingly well, starting with the 1948-

49 season and staying with the Braves until the 1954-55 season. His statistics show he was a leading scorer for the Quebec league, with an impressive record for goals and assists. Coach Toe Blake considered Larry his star player.

Kwong became a legend in the Quebec Senior League. He was among the league's top scorers from his first season, where he scored eighty-four points in sixty-three games. Next season in 1949-50 he earned sixty points for twenty-four goals and thirty-five assists in sixty games. In 1951, he won the league's Byng of Vimy Trophy for Most Valuable Player. That year, as the team's assistant captain, he led the Braves to the league title, and to the Alexander Cup for the Canadian Major Senior Hockey Championship.

Winning the Lady Byng trophy for Most Valuable Player was a highlight of Kwong's career.

As well, his statistics for penalties were impressively good. As a power forward, Kwong was in an excellent position to score goals and set up his teammates to score. Yet somehow his energetic performance on the ice didn't lead to the kind of violence that earns players a lot of penalties. He spent very little time in the penalty box. For some of his seasons, you could count the number of penalty minutes on one hand — and still have fingers left over! This kind of clean playing record contrasts strongly with the average performance in senior hockey leagues. Many players would rack up in a single game as many penalties for hooking, high-sticking, or even fighting as Kwong earned in an entire season.

Good as Gretzky

Kwong was a hero in the Quebec Senior Hockey League, praised by his coach Toe Blake in the sports pages of newspapers. Quebec journalists called him 'The China Clipper' and *le petit Chinois*. The Valleyfield Braves and their star player were featured in the sports pages of many newspapers, and not just their hometown paper. For one game against Chicoutimi, the Braves won four to one. Larry assisted on his team's first goal, and scored a hat trick as "the starry Valleyfield center" according to Canadian Press wire service.

A trading card shows Larry Kwong with the Assistant Captain emblem on his Valleyfield Braves jersey.

He competed against Jacques Plante, Jean Beliveau and other players who went on to play for NHL teams and later be honoured with places in the NHL Hockey Hall of Fame.

"Larry made his wing men look good because he was a great passer," said Jean Beliveau as quoted by journalist Kevin Mitchell. "He was doing what a center man is supposed to do."

Years after his time in Quebec, Kwong received high praise from the author of a book on the history of the Valleyfield Braves. Gaston Legault de Coteau-du-Lac didn't hesitate to compare *le petit Chinois* with a later hockey legend. "He was an exceptional player," wrote the well-known chronicler. "He was smart enough to get himself behind the opposing team's goal in order to make effective passes. At this level, he was as good as Gretzky."

A portrait in his Braves uniform shows Larry Kwong as a confident and handsome young man.

Two China Clippers

It's still not clear exactly who in Vernon bestowed the nickname 'The China Clipper' on Larry Kwong. Though in the 21st century calling someone the China Clipper would seem racist and inappropriate, at the time this was considered a friendly sports nickname. Certainly sports journalists used the name when reporting on both Larry Kwong and another Chinese-Canadian athlete. In the Canadian Football League (CFL), Normie Kwong was playing football for the Edmonton Eskimos. In 1948, the same year Larry Kwong played for the NHL, the Eskimos won the CFL's Grey Cup with eighteen-year-old Normie Kwong, the youngest player ever for a Grey Cup-winning team. It was a time when racial prejudice was being faced and challenged across Canada, and in major league sports in many countries. Sometimes the challenges were successful. And certainly, no one pretended either of these young men weren't fine athletes.

Investing His Income

Earning a stable income meant Kwong had more than just enough money to live on — he had enough to invest in a business. Like many Chinese-Canadians, he knew restaurants could be reliable businesses. It wasn't long before he became the proud owner of a restaurant in the Besner building on Rue Sainte-Cécile in Valleyfield.

He enjoyed owning a restaurant where his friends could come and he could meet people. It was a pleasure to eat his meals in his own restaurant, so he ate there every day he was home in Valleyfield. His presence there became a real attraction, drawing regular customers who enjoyed his company and the service in his restaurant. He was proud of how nice the place looked, with its checkered wallpaper. Business was steady and the company was good.

He even began to speak a little French. As a young man in Trail he had wanted to learn French to be like Mr. Kerr, the owner of the Crown Point Hotel who was willing to give him a job. Now he was living that dream, too.

Many of the employees became his friends. One of the waitresses in particular thought very highly of her boss; Janine Boyer not only waited tables but kept the books for the restaurant. Kwong had never thought of himself as a good student in school, and though he was a good businessman he needed assistance with the paperwork. Looking back on this time in his life, Kwong has said little about his friendship with Janine, but his grown daughter suggests warmly that

Janine was his girlfriend at the time. Janine became a good friend of not only Larry but of his sister Ina and his brother Jack. She even kept up acquaintance with them years later.

The Valleyfield Braves team is shown here, celebrating their winning the Canadian Championship.

Friends and Colleagues

Playing in Quebec offered Kwong something he really valued: colleagues who became his lifelong friends. Wherever he went in life, he always made contacts with people who thought well of him and were glad to stay in touch. In Quebec, though, he had friends like teammate André Corriveau who became a business partner. Two of his closest friends were Georges Bougie and Jean-Paul Bisaillon; these friends have kept in touch ever since their time on the team.

There are photos on the walls of Kwong's home and in his photo albums, showing his slim, youthful figure at golf courses with his friends, or riding in their cars. While he did enjoy golf, tennis was his summer sport for keeping fit in the off season months. Games with champion players and Wimbledon winners showed that Kwong was more than just a recreational player.

"I loved my years spent at Valleyfield," he later told a Quebec journalist. "That city became my second home."

On the ice, a number of times Kwong would face off against Herb Carnegie playing for the Sherbrooke St Francis or Quebec Aces teams. Carnegie had much in common with Kwong, though he was a little taller and was born in Ontario four years before Kwong. As a black man born in Ontario, Carnegie faced some of the same challeges Kwong did as a professional player. Though some teammates or opponents held racist views, there were many reliable teammates and colleagues for both men. And both had the same experience of being offered more money to play for a team in the Quebec Senior Hockey League than for the New York Rovers. Just after Kwong left the Rovers in 1948, Carnegie was scouted by them. Rovers management told Carnegie that if he signed with them, he would make international headlines. "My family can't eat headlines," was Carnegie's reply, as he later wrote in his autobiography. He turned down their three offers of pay that didn't match what he'd been earning in the QSHL, and like Kwong, enjoyed a good career in the senior leagues.

Changing Times

As time went on, there were further career shifts for Larry Kwong. When his coach Toe Blake left the Braves in 1955 to become head coach for the Montreal Canadiens, it was time for Kwong to move on as well. He took an offer from the Trois-Rivières Lions for the 1955-56 season, then went on to play for the Troy Bruins in the International Hockey League for the last half of the season and part of the next year. The last half of the 1956-57 season he played for the Cornwall Chevies in the Ontario Senior Hockey Association. It was interesting to play for different teams, and see what different approaches they brought to the game.

While playing in Ontario, Kwong was approached by a representative from the Panthers hockey team in Nottingham, England. Would he come to England and be a player and a coach for the Panthers? Going to England meant overseas travel, as his father had done to come to Canada. It sounded like a good idea, and Kwong resolved to take the Panthers' offer. I'll go and try it for a year, he told himself. In the end, he stayed in Europe not for one year, but for fifteen.

Chapter 8: A Sportsman in Europe

A team photo of the Nottingham Panthers shows Larry Kwong among his teammates.

WITH HIS BRITISH contract, Kwong became the first professional hockey player from BC to play overseas. He was hired to play for the Panthers, a team based in Nottingham in the East Midlands area of England. He set out to do his best.

Photos from that time show Kwong wearing a number 6 jersey. In the 1957-58 season, he scored fifty-five goals in fifty-five games. He was a sensation on the ice, and celebrated in the sports pages of the newspapers. A goal judge for the British league, Baz Shaw, said in the video *The Longest Shot:* "Superstar is not enough to describe Kwong."

Leaving the Restaurant Behind

When Kwong accepted an offer to play hockey in Britain, he shared the news with his brothers and sisters. This was a good opportunity, and he was leaving Valleyfield to play for the Panthers. But what should he do with the restaurant he owned in Valleyfield? It was agreed among the family that Larry shouldn't sell the restaurant until he knew how reliable his position would be with the team in Nottingham. After all, since leaving the Braves he had played for three other teams in two seasons. "I'll try it for a year and see how it goes," was the way he explained his decision in later years. Kwong's brother Jim came to Valleyfield and lived there for a year to run the restaurant.

By the time a year had passed, it was clear to Kwong he didn't need to keep the restaurant as a safety net. He wanted to live in Europe for a while, and he had an offer to consider. The regular customers who had enjoyed his presence felt the place just wasn't the same without him. When Kwong returned briefly to Canada for a visit, it was clear the restaurant was not prospering in the same way without his daily presence. The restaurant was sold in 1958, and his brother Jim returned to his own home in the western provinces. It had been a good experience for Kwong to be a business owner, and at least one of his former employees remembered him fondly for years afterwards.

Someone Special

Nottingham held other interests for Kwong besides hockey. It was where he met Audrey Coven and got to know her. Six years younger than Larry, Audrey had a deep interest in dance and the opera. After finishing her school years, she trained and worked as a hairdresser. Meeting this trim, muscular athlete made a terrific impression on her. He was more than just a hockey star to her, he was a man with energy and enthusiasm who played tennis as his summer sport, and sometimes golf as well. She was so impressed by this traveller from the distant colonies with his foreign looks and Canadian accent.

He was different from anyone she knew — a sports hero and an international success. There were over three hundred thousand people living in Nottingham at the time, but only one man like Larry Kwong. It's no wonder they fell in love.

A photo from Larry Kwong's time in Nottingham shows his determination and his athletic good looks.

A New Offer

While playing for the Panthers, Kwong was approached by a representative of a hockey league in Switzerland with an offer to help them develop and improve the league. Kwong always left his options open, so he was free to leave the English team. He wanted to travel more and see the world. It was a good time for him to go to Switzerland.

In the 1958-59 season, Kwong played in the newly-formed Swiss League. It's no surprise he became the first professional coach of Chinese descent for hockey in that country. In fact, HC Ambri-Piotta were the first team anywhere in the world to hire a person of Chinese descent to be their coach. It's also no surprise he was the leading scorer for his team. As a playing coach, he was later involved with Lugano and Lausanne teams as well as Ambri-Piotta. He made major contributions to the emerging sport of hockey in Switzerland, from 1958 to 1964. All the Swiss rinks were outdoors, which suited Kwong well. It reminded him of his youth, skating on frozen ponds and rough home-made ice.

This photo shows Larry Kwong on the left, playing hard for Ambri-Piotta in 1958.

Even in Switzerland, far from his birthplace, there were ties linking Kwong to his past. His past as a Smoke Eater meant something to hockey people here where the World Championship Tournaments were played. He was instrumental in developing the emerging Swiss

Hockey league, as his former teammate Mike Buckna (a fellow Smoke Eater) was for the Czech National Hockey Team. Known as the 'Father of Czech Hockey,' Buckna had an even bigger impact in that country than Kwong did in Switzerland. Between the World Championship and the Olympic Games, there were a number of opportunities for positive interactions among teams and coaches.

By 1961 when the Smoke Eaters once again represented Canada at the World Hockey Championships, Kwong was an active part of the hosting in Lausanne and Geneva. He met with his fellow Smoke Eaters as they made a tour of exhibition games. At the end of the tournament, the Smoke Eaters defeated the Soviet team to take their second Wor

Travelling

One of the joys of Kwong's life was travelling. Each summer from 1958 to 1964, he took a trans-Atlantic passenger ship back to Canada. With pride, he brought Audrey to Canada to meet his family. The ship carried them first of all to New York City, where he took Audrey on a tour and showed her all the places he had known.

It was while walking past an automobile dealership that a convertible caught his eye. It was new, and powder-blue with beautiful smooth lines. He had never wanted to own any car like he suddenly wanted that one. "I wish that I could buy that car," he said to Audrey, as he steeled himself to turn and walk away from the dealership.

"Why don't you buy that car?" Audrey suggested gently. He'd never even considered such an idea before. Years later, telling the story, his voice broke as he spoke of realizing how much how she supported him in buying this fine vehicle, and how much she cared for him. Men born in the time and place that he was did not learn a lot of flowery romantic talk. The way he was raised, it wasn't proper to speak much to others about the feelings one has for a wife — but the feelings were strong.

Together in the new car, they drove west, touring parts of Canada and the United States as he took Audrey to Calgary to meet his family. They took a different route back to the East Coast. When they boarded the ship to return to Europe, the car was loaded by crane;

Kwong took a photo of it swinging as he watched anxiously from the ship's deck. For the rest of the years they lived in Switzerland, he drove that convertible and maintained it with pride.

He and Audrey were married in the spring of 1964, when he was beginning work in Switzerland as the tennis coach and teacher at a Catholic school for girls in Lausanne. Not far from Geneva, Lausanne is in the part of Switzerland where French is spoken. It was a modest-sized city, about a third the size of Audrey's home city Nottingham. After their daughter was born in 1968, Audrey was a stay-at-home mother, but she kept up her interest in dance and the opera.

"What will we do after hockey is finished?" Kwong and colleague Gaston Pelletier asked each other. For a while, they both went to school in Lausanne with Audrey, and learned hairdressing. It was good to have another skill available for the future.

His sister Ina and his brother Jack came to Switzerland for a visit. He was able to drive them on tours of the countryside with pride, showing them his fine car and the home he and Audrey had made. During the Olympics, his friend Janine Boyer came as well to visit them and little Kristina.

Teaching at the Catholic school for girls was surprisingly interesting. He was a sports coach and gave tennis lessons at the school. During eight years working there, Kwong was living part of a dream he'd begun to realize in Quebec, one he had since working as a bellhop for the hotel in Trail, BC. He was speaking French, just as he'd resolved to learn one day to be like the hotel owner he admired.

In 1968, a few years before the landmark Canada/Russian hockey series in 1972, Larry Kwong was on a team of expatriate Swiss-Canadians that played an exhibition game with the Olympic champion Soviet team. The Soviets had just won gold at the Winter Olympics in Grenoble, France. Kwong and his team won that exhibition game, as well as many tournaments against the best national teams and hockey clubs in Europe.

Chapter 9: Calgary Grocer

At his brother Jack's request, after fifteen years in Europe, Kwong returned to Canada to manage the family grocery business — a much expanded business — in Calgary. His brother was able to retire, and brother Larry was able to take on a new kind of work. Living in Canada again came as a welcome change, instead of visiting.

When Larry Kwong returned to Canada in 1972, he brought his English-born wife Audrey and their Swiss-born daughter. Little Kristina was four years old at the time, and it wasn't long before she was ready for kindergarten and school. Gradually her accent shifted from her mother's Nottingham tones to a Canadian accent like her cousins and classmates and her father. Audrey settled in as a mother and found much to interest her in music and dance in their new home city. Meanwhile, Kwong adjusted to work as a businessman supervising many employees in a small chain of grocery stores named Food-Vale.

In retirement from professional sports, Kwong was luckier than many former hockey players. The only old hockey injury that had lingering effects for Kwong's health was an elbow injury. It would trouble him from time to time, especially in cold weather.

Though he had moved on to his new career managing the grocery chain, amateur sports remained an important part of the Kwong family life. The love of sports was carried on in his daughter Kristina. "I think I was born with skates on and a racquet in my hands," says his daughter. "My dad taught me to play tennis and hockey. We belonged to the tennis club. In the winter we'd always be outside playing. The school would flood the grounds and make a rink." Kwong and his daughter would play there, or he'd take her to the frozen Bow River and teach her how to skate there. He took his sister Betty Chan's daughter too, who was three years older than Kristina. "You learn to skate on that kind of ice, you'll be a better skater," he told both the girls.

Chatting informally years later, Kwong's daughter reminisced about her childhood, and not being allowed candy as a child: "We never had it in the house," she said. "Now my kids go to my dad's place and he makes sure that several candy dishes are well stocked with their favourite candy."

A Football Connection

An unexpected result of moving to Calgary was the opportunity for Larry Kwong to meet retired football player Normie Kwong, years after 1948 when they had each been the first Chinese-Canadians playing in their professional leagues. Though the two men were unrelated, they had similar backgrounds in many ways, and similar outlooks on life. They became friends, and when Larry offered to teach Normie's sons to play tennis, the idea was welcome. Perhaps his coaching was some kind of influence, but the younger son, Brad, went on to play hockey. As an undergraduate, Brad became captain of the hockey team at Harvard University.

Brad has a story to tell about his own time as a professional hockey player in Europe after playing for Harvard. "There was a time in San Moritz, a group of fans came down, said hello, and said they knew my father." This surprised Brad, for while his father was understandably famous among fans of Canadian football, his fame couldn't be expected to amount to much in Switzerland. In a few more words, everything became clear. These were hockey fans of

Larry Kwong during his career in Switzerland, and they thought that Brad must be his son.

"I had to giggle at the story," said Larry Kwong's daughter Kristina. She had faced some similar assumptions when her family moved to Calgary. "Growing up I was always asked if I was Normie's daughter."

Normie Kwong has gone on to be awarded the Order of Canada for his achievements in sports, and in 2005 he became Alberta's Lieutenant-Governor. Getting to know Normie was part of what made Larry Kwong a fan of Canadian football — and he still buys season tickets to the Calgary Stampeders. He's had them every year since he was fifty-five. Even in Calgary's winter weather, he never used to miss a home game, according to his daughter.

Loss and Links

It was in 1979 Kwong lost his wife Audrey to cancer. He has little to say about this difficult time, but it seems his family ties were what brought him through this profound loss. Perhaps this loss is part of why he has continued to be connected and helpful to his relatives. Certainly it's one of the reasons his sisters Betty and Ina, in particular, have taken care to keep an eye on him and be part of his daughter's life.

"You can always talk to him," said his sister-in-law Janet Jang in Chad Soon's film on Kwong. "He's quite understanding, and he's willing to help at any time. I think we've come a long ways since the old days. Everybody's more accepting, and you're part of the Canadian community." As a member of the Chamber of Commerce, Kwong certainly became part of the community in Calgary. He also joined the Rotary Club, forming social connections and friendships that have lasted through decades of meetings and projects.

Well Matched

Entertainer Bill Cosby was in Calgary for a show in November of 1983, and he wanted to play tennis while he was here. "I guess Bill Cosby's people contacted the tennis club we belong to and asked the manager of the club to arrange a partner for Bill," is how Kwong's grown daughter Kristina tells the story. "Specifically they asked for someone 'really good.' Right away the club called Larry and he gratefully accepted the challenge."

Because of Bill Cosby's fame as a comedian and a joker, Kwong thought the game would be all fun and laughs. Instead, their game turned out to be a serious two hour match. Kwong hadn't known that in university, Cosby was trained in physical education and had learned to take sports seriously. At one point, Cosby had expected to have a career as a gym teacher. It's odd to think these two very different men have common experience in coaching. It's odder still to imagine them facing off across the net.

"I remember my dad saying after the game that was one of the toughest matches he'd ever played," recalled Kristina. "I wanted to skip school that day to go to the club to watch, but my dad made me go to school." Luckily for young Kristina, what her father thought was going to be a simple game for an hour or less turned out to last two hours. She was able to go to the club after school and watch the rest of the match. The competition kept up, unflagging, till the final point was scored.

"I remember thinking as I was watching how good a player Bill Cosby was," said Kristina. "I can see why my dad said that was a tough match. I don't remember who won," she added wistfully. Her father remembers. He won that match, and later went to see Cosby's show. What Kristina is certain of is that Cosby, who was aged forty-six at the time of the game, never realized his opponent was sixty years old.

Oldtimers Hockey

While living in Calgary, Kwong played hockey in an Oldtimers league. Becoming friends with his teammates, playing hard in a recreational league — these were good things in a good life. For years he played with the same men, keeping fit and connected to each other's lives. "He was always in motion," says his daughter Kristina, remembering the years when she was an active teenager and her dad was an active man playing tennis as well as hockey.

As well as the good memories, there's a moment that affected Kwong deeply. During one game, he was watching from the bench when a good friend collapsed on the ice. It was a heart attack, and in spite of prompt attention the friend later died. The profound impact of this moment was never forgotten by Kwong, who hadn't really seen himself as aging. The loss of his friend brought back memories of his old Rovers coach Fred Metcalfe, who had a heart attack during a game and later died aged only forty-three. When Kwong began to have symptoms of angina, he went to the doctor. Gradually, he began slowing down his physical activities, and eventually stopped playing vigorous sports so much, at age sixty-six.

Moving On

Two of Kwong's sisters, Kate and Ina, spoke to him around the time he began slowing down. It seemed to them their brother had been alone for a while. It had been nearly ten years since his wife Audrey had passed away, and his daughter Kristina was grown. They were concerned he was lonely.

"You know, we still keep in touch with Janine," said his sister Ina. She and Kate worked in San Francisco as secretaries for 'bigwig' businessmen. Janine Boyer had moved to San Francisco also, and was working in a restaurant there. Maybe there was a little encouragement from Larry's sisters, but however it happened, in 1988 Janine came to Calgary for the Olympics. And of course, to visit Larry.

So it was that he came to have a second marriage — to the girlfriend from his time in Quebec, Janine Boyer. In 1989, they were married, and Janine came to live with him in Alberta.

By age seventy, Kwong could still pass for fifty. A lifetime of sports activities kept him looking athletic. With his wife Janine, he was living about half an hour out of Calgary to the southwest, in a town near a golf course in the foothills. He took up golf about 1989, and took to it as well as he had tennis, or track and field, or hockey. It was a good sport for recovery from surgery, when he had a heart valve replaced. By 1994 he had a golf handicap of eighteen — a respectable handicap for any retired gentleman to maintain for years, especially one who was the survivor of two triple bypass operations on his heart.

His heart recovered from that surgery, and then had to recover again from the loss of Janine. She shared her life with Larry Kwong for more than ten years, until she passed away from cancer in 1999.

Reunions

A family that starts with fifteen children is likely to grow. In 1993, the scattered descendants of Ng Shu Kwong's fifteen children gathered in Vernon for a family reunion. Sixty-seven of them turned out for a summer party that brought back memories and made new ones. Some of these relatives use the surname Eng, others use Kwong, and the rest have taken the family names of the men who married some of the nine daughters of Ng Shu Kwong. Many of the relatives gathered again in Calgary during June of 2013 for Larry Kwong's ninetieth birthday celebration, with over two hundred guests gathered including friends. But of all his many relatives, he takes special pride in his two granddaughters. There's more than looks and genes in common in this part of the family, there's the love of athletic activities. While his little granddaughters aren't budding hockey stars, they are dancers and in their quick, controlled movements you can see his same drive, energy, and enjoyment.

Hard News

The biggest physical challenge Kwong had to handle came late in life, in his eighties. By then he was twice a widower, and the survivor of cardiac surgery. Diabetes was taking its toll on him. "The doctor told me, `If you want to live long enough to see your granddaughters go to school, I have to take your leg off,'" he later told journalist David Davis. "I tell you, that hit me like a rock.... But I'm all right now. I just had to go through that." The powerful right knee on which he used to pivot, turning on the ice, was no longer able to bear him past all challenges.

Before the year was out, both of Kwong's lower legs were amputated. With physiotherapy and careful practise, he learned to walk again on prosthetics. He keeps active and goes out to meet with friends, but spending time with his granddaughters is a particular joy for him. As time goes on, he makes use of a wheelchair to reduce chances of injury from falling.

Chapter 10: Hall of Fame

This living pioneer turned ninety years old in 2013. Kwong has outlived both his first wife and his second, and diabetes has taken both his lower legs, but he is still alert and active in retirement with a second career managing his family's chain of grocery stores. He lives in Calgary now, with a caregiver who keeps house and assists him when he needs it. He was still working out three times a week, and proud he could walk with his prosthetic legs.

There's a running joke going around the Kwong family and friends about cold feet. Kwong's grown daughter Kristina says it dates back to the first winter after her father lost his feet. "My dad had just had his surgeries earlier that year. Your brain plays a lot of tricks on you after you have had limbs amputated," she explained. "We were at a football game and it was chilly. My feet were freezing. I made a comment to my dad about how cold my feet were. He looked a bit surprised and said, 'Your feet are cold? That's funny, mine aren't cold at all.'"

At first, Kristina thought he was kidding, till she looked at him. "I realized by the look on his face that he was serious," so she replied back, in something of a joking manner but also kind of serious:

"That's cause you have no feet." Because he has such a good sense of humour, he laughed at himself for forgetting.

In his private collection, Larry Kwong still has his jersey from his time playing for the Trail Smoke Eaters.

The cold no longer troubles Kwong the same way it did when he was a young dockworker in Nanaimo, playing for the Clippers at night. And now he has what his daughter calls 'a standing joke' with family and friends at Calgary football or hockey games. "Friends will stop by our seats to say hi," according to Kristina. "He will always ask if their feet are cold and laugh, saying 'mine are fine'!"

Public Recognition

There has been some public recognition of Larry Kwong in recent years. Over the decades since his career as an athlete and coach, his story had faded into obscurity. It took a long time for him to be recognized. In 1997 he was invited back to Switzerland to be honoured for his contributions to the Swiss hockey league. Then in 2001, he returned to Valleyfield to be feted at the fifty-year-reunion of the Alexander Cup-winning team. The celebration in Quebec included a banquet and a parade.

Several journalists, students and even film-makers are showcasing features that promote recognition of Larry Kwong's career achievements. Some of the recognition has been happening in his hometown of Calgary. In 2002, he was honoured with Calgary's Asian Heritage Month Award, not only for his sports history but for his contributions to the community. At age eighty-one, he played a round in the Peter Gzowski Invitational golf tournament, which is a prestigious fundraiser for literacy and was held in Calgary in 2004. On March 20, 2008, Kwong was the guest of honour at a Calgary Flames hockey game, receiving a salute on the Saddledome's JumboTron for breaking the NHL's colour barrier sixty years earlier.

Other moments of recognition are based in the Okanagan Valley, his boyhood home. Mission Hill Elementary School in Vernon was proud to welcome Larry Kwong to their school on March 27, 2009. Students celebrated him as a member in their school's Hall of Fame as a hockey pioneer, and a champion of diversity and fair play for all. The school has many multicultural murals. That day, the students' posters were on display with slogans like 'You Can't Stop the China Clipper' and 'No More Colour Barriers – Thank You Larry' as Kwong addressed the students, talking about his life and some of the things he had seen change.

Kwong had actually had a bad fall on arriving in Vernon and was rushed to the local hospital's Emergency Room for treatment of arm lacerations and a suspected concussion. But in true old-time hockey style, he didn't let that stop him from making his engagements.

Shown at centre ice in Vernon with his caregiver Fima, Larry Kwong salutes the crowd.

Later that same day, Larry Kwong was celebrated at Wesbild Centre in Vernon. He was the celebrity dropping the puck at the game between the Vernon Vipers and the Salmon Arm Silverbacks. There was polite applause when he was introduced, but when the announcer declared he was the first hockey player from the Okanagan Valley to play in the NHL, the home-town crowd leapt to its feet and cheered. And when Kwong received the Heritage Award from the Society of North American Hockey Historians and Researchers (SONAHR), they cheered again.

Trevor Linden and Larry Kwong are shown with their awards at the 2010 BC Hockey Hall of Fame dinner.

Among the current and retired hockey players who have met Larry Kwong in recent years, Gordie Howe stands out. One of the best players as well as one of the most gracious, he treated Kwong as a peer when they met at an awards ceremony. There have been other moments of public recognition, but that one was particularly satisfying.

In 2013, Larry Kwong was inducted into the BC Sports Hall of Fame in the Pioneer category. Being inducted into the Hall of Fame wasn't an automatic process. He was nominated in the new category of Pioneer, and the adjudication took some time. It didn't hurt that in 2010 the Okanagan Hockey School honoured him with their own inaugural Pioneer Award, or that in 2011 he was accepted into the Okanagan Sports Hall of Fame. As well, in Penticton, BC in 2010, Kwong was celebrated as a Pioneer at a BC Hockey Hall of Fame dinner. As the award was announced, the first to shake Kwong's hand at the ceremony was Pat Quinn, NHL player and coach, and NHL player Trevor Linden rushed through the crowd as well. For the BC Sports Hall of Fame, testimonials from other hockey legends and professionals were acquired to support the nomination.

"I remember Larry Kwong very well," Jean Beliveau told nominator Chad Soon in a telephone interview. "It brings back great memories. He was a very good player. You could see he enjoyed playing the game. He was a very smooth player – very skilled, with a beautiful style. I support his nomination for the Pioneer Award. He deserves it."

"He was a special player," said legendary sports journalist Red Fisher to Chad Soon. "I remember him well from the times I covered Royals-Braves games at the Forum. I remember the high regard Royals players had for him as a player and human being. I remember him with fondness and respect now."

Chad Soon also spoke with Hockey Canada President Bob Nicholson, who stated: "There are very few figures in Canadian hockey that have made an impact like that of Mr. Kwong.... Mr Kwong battled through ethnic barriers and stereotypes throughout his long career, and handled each and every situation with class and dignity."

"The NHL has produced many stories of individuals with determination to break down barriers and with perseverance to overcome obstacles, but Larry Kwong's story is such a tremendous example of those qualities," Calgary Flames President Ken King wrote in a letter of support. "Mr. Kwong has the qualities and character that force open eyes and doors, resulting in a better sport and a better world."

There are other highlights in the public recognition of Larry Kwong's exciting sports career. He was featured prominently in the award-winning documentary *Lost Years: a People's Struggle for Justice* (2011) by Kenda Gee and Tom Radford. Later that year, Kwong was the lone Chinese-Canadian to be included in a trading card set of 100 great Canadians called In The Game's Canadiana. The next year, he became a comic book hero in David H.T. Wong's *Escape to Gold Mountain: A Graphic History of the Chinese in North America.*

Sixty-six years after he suited up for that single NHL game, the New York Rangers finally honoured Kwong. In July 2014, Rangers scout Ernie Gare presented Kwong with a personalized jersey sent by Glen Sather at the world theatrical premiere of *The Shift: The Story of the China Clipper* (2013), a documentary by Chester Sit, Wes Miron, and Tracey Nagai.

Though the Hockey Hall of Fame in Toronto has not inducted Kwong as a member, it has accepted a jersey of his for display. The wool jersey worn by Kwong when playing for the Nanaimo Clippers is on display in the Hall, one sample of his long and successful playing and coaching career.

Social Media

With a modest presence in social media, Kwong has both an e-mail address and a Facebook account. His caregiver assists him to some extent with his correspondence, both postal and electronic, as does his daughter.

"He has kept in touch with people from organizations everywhere," says Kristina. "He has friends all over the world." To the few articles in recent years about his hockey experiences, he has responded humbly and simply. When invited, he has done school visits promoting awareness of how his life has transformed as times have changed.

"I can understand the sports writers might want to write a little article about me. Sport is their business," he commented in an unguarded moment. "But a film? And a book? I can't understand all this attention." To Kwong, his life has been nothing unusual, just ordinary work from an ordinary man. It's been a good life, and a very plain one, nothing to make a big fuss about, he says.

And yet he has organised photo albums full of memories — *five* big albums. These albums are filled with sorted and arranged images, winnowed down from a lifetime's collection to make an impressive body of work. His birth certificate is there, along with his mother's immigration papers. There are telegrams also in the albums, conveying the news when he was accepted to play for the Rangers' farm team, and word from the bank when he was paying for a house for his mother. As well, pictures from his childhood and work and travels have been collected to display on his shelves. Many framed photographs hang on his walls, showing family and friends in proud moments. One particular frame holds an enlarged photo, a fine shot of the beloved powder-blue convertible he drove for years. It will be a lucky archivist who gets to receive the eventual donation of Kwong's papers as reference materials for archival purposes.

In his nineties, Kwong still meets with his friends from the Rotary club every week. Over coffee, they sit together and share what's going on in their lives. You're never really out of Rotary, it seems. He also continues to keep in touch with his former teammates from the Oldtimers hockey league. The men enjoy getting together for coffee and conversation, though there are fewer of them gathering as time goes on.

Television has become one of his pastimes. With his sister-in-law Janet, he shares an interest in *Dancing With the Stars* and similar shows. During the 2014 Winter Olympics, Kwong kept an eye on the hockey games and shared with his daughter their interest in the women's hockey games in particular. It was Olympic gold for the Canadian team, and the bronze medal for the Swiss team. The man who helped grow the Swiss Hockey League and who taught his daughter to skate shared in her Olympic enthusiasm that winter. And he watches in person and on home videos as his granddaughters dance.

Timeline

1895 Kwong Hing Lung general store began business in Vernon, BC as a general store owned and operated by Ng Shu Kwong and his family

1923 Larry Kwong born in Vernon, BC.

1936 Started playing hockey with the Hydrophones, won the BC Midget Championships at age 16

1939 - 1941 Played for the Vernon Hydrophones, won the 1941 BC Juvenile Championships at age 18

1941-42 season played for Trail Smoke Eaters

1942-43 Nanaimo Clippers

1943-44 Vancouver St Regis

1944-45 Red Deer Wheelers in the Central Garrison League

1945-46 Trail Smoke Eaters

1946-47 and 1947-48 seasons played for the New York Rovers

March 13, 1948 played one game for the New York Rangers

1948-49 through 1954-55 seasons played for Valleyfield Braves in Quebec

1955-56 season played for Troy Bruins in the IHL

1955-56 season played for Trois Rivieres Lions in QHL

1956-57 season played for Cornwall Chevies in OHASr league

1956-57 season played for Troy Bruins

1957-58 played in Britain for the Nottingham Panthers

1958-64 player/coach in Switzerland for hockey clubs Amber-Piotta, Lugano, and Lausanne

1964 tennis coach for Swiss private school

1972 returned to Calgary to run family business

1994 in retirement, returned to playing golf

References

Beliveau, Jean. "Larry Kwong Appreciation Society" *Facebook.com.* Posted May 26, 2010. Retrieved August 19, 2010.

Brooklyn Daily Eagle. October 22, 1946, p12. Retrieved August 10, 2014. http://www.newspapers.com/newspage/55027132/

Canadian Press CP. "Valleyfield Wins When Kwong Gets Three." "Larry Kwong: The Longest Shot." *YouTube.* Posted July 27, 2010. Retrieved September 2, 2013. http://www.youtube.com/watch?v=HpUeWY2ldfs

Carnegie, Herb. *A Fly in a Pail of Milk: the Herb Carnegie Story.* Toronto, ON: Mosaic Adult, 1996.

Carrier, Roch. *The Hockey Sweater.* Toronto, ON: House of Anansi Press, 1979.

Colletti, Al. "Ex-Regina Mentor Tries For U.S. Army." *Montreal Gazette,* Feb. 3, 1942. Vol. CLXXL No 29, p 14.

Cox, Damien. "NHL Lockout: Old-timers don't resent today's money." *The Star.com.* Web. Posted November 22, 2012. Retrieved November 30. http://www.thestar.com/sports/hockey/2012/11/22/

nhl_lockout_oldtimers_caught_in_crossfire_dont_resent_todays_money_cox.html

Davis, David. "A Hockey Pioneer's Moment." *New York Times*. February 19, 2013. Retrieved November 12, 2013. http://www.nytimes/com/2013/02/20/sports/hockey/larry-kwongs-shift-for-rangers-in-1947-48-broke-a-barrier.html?ref=sports&_r=0

Douglas, William. "From Larry Kwong to Brad Kwong: Celebrating Hockey's Rich Asian Heritage." *The Colour of Hockey*. Web. Posted April 4, 2014. Retrieved June 6, 2014. http://colorofhockey.com/2014/04/04/from-larry-kwong-to-brad-kwong-celebrating-hockeys-rich-asian-legacy/#comments

Fischler, Stan. *Behind the Net: 101 Incredible Hockey Stories*. New York, NY: Skyhorse Publishing, 2013, p129-30.

Fullerton, Hugh, Jr. "Roundup: Hockey Makes Progressive Move in Naming Fred Metcalfe." *Milwaukee Journal*. March 25, 1946, p2.

Gee, Kenda D. "First Star In The Game Of Life: The Live & Times Of Hockey Hero Larry Kwong." *Chinacity*. January-February 1994, pp 8-9. Posted November 20, 2008. Retrieved September 1, 2010. http://everything2.com/title/Larry+Kwong

Hawthorne, Tom. "Hockey Gentleman was known as 'Beaver.'" *The Globe and Mail*. May 5, 2014, pS10.

Hawthorne, Tom. "Larry Kwong beat long odds." The Globe and Mail. January 23, 2008.

"Larry Kwong: The Longest Shot." *YouTube*. Posted July 27, 2010. Retrieved September 2, 2010. http://www.youtube.com/watch?v=HpUeWY2ldfs

MacGregor, Roy. "Now is the time to save the game." *The Globe and Mail*. September 14, 2013, pS8.

Maki, Allan. "Shifting Ice." *The Globe and Mail*. September 14, 2013, pS6.

Mitchell, Kevin. "Larry Kwong." *Vernon Morning Star*. February 24, 2013: pA21.

Price, John and Sonia Manak. "Panama Maru incident shook Ottawa and B.C." *Victoria Times-Colonist.* October 17, 2013, p A11.

Soon, Chad. "Larry Kwong: A Hero Comes Home part 2." *YouTube. com.* Posted May 25, 2009. Retrieved September 2, 2010. http://www.youtube.com/watch?B8o5ojA2hD4&feature=related

Soon, Chad. "Hockey Hero Larry Kwong." *YouTube.com.* Posted February 11, 2009. Retrieved September 2, 2010. http://www.youtube.com/watch?v=Z-cPkT6Jquw&NR=1

Soon, Chad. "The Return of King Kwong, Part II." *SONAHR Canada.* http://sonahrsports.com/the-return-of-king-kwong-part-ii-p151-107htm originally published in *Insider's Edge Magazine* November & December 2009. http://www.mondaymag.com/news/135927658.html

Théorêt, Hugues. "À 80 ans, Larry Kwong a encore le logo des Braves tatoué sur le coeur." *Hebdos Regionaux — Monteregies. Le Soleil de Salaberry de Valleyfield,* Valleyfield QC. May 1, 2004. Retrieved July 14, 2014. http://www.hebdosregionaux.ca/monteregie/2004/05/01/a-80-ans-larry-kwong-a-encore-le-logo-des-braves-tatoue-sur-le-coeur

Woolsey, Garth. "Mr Hockey teams up with a worthy cause." *Toronto Star.* Web. April 2, 2009. Retrieved on November 30, 2014. http://www.thestar.com/opinion/columnists/2009/04/02/mr_hockey_teams_up_with_a_worthy_cause.html

Zisman, Alan. Note on house deed in Vancouver. *Facebook.com.* Posted August 27, 2014.

About the Author

A lifelong hockey fan, Paula Johanson has written more than two dozen books, including the biographies *Lady Gaga* and *Lance Armstrong* from Greenwood Publishing, *Fish: From The Catch To Your Table* from Rosen Publishing's series *The Truth About The Food Supply*, *Love Poetry: Let Me Count The Ways* from Enslow Publishers, and her novel *Tower in the Crooked Wood* from Five Rivers Publishing.

Johanson was shortlisted twice for the Prix Aurora Award for Canadian science fiction writing, while raising gifted twins on an organic-method small farm. An accredited teacher, she has edited curriculum educational materials for the Alberta Distance Learning Centre and eTraffic Solutions.

Books by Five Rivers

Sir John Abbott
Sir John Thompson
Sir Mackenzie Bowell
Sir Charles Tupper
Sir Wilfred Laurier
Sir Robert Borden
Arthur Meighen
William Lyon Mackenzie King
R. B. Bennett
Louis St. Laurent
John Diefenbaker
Lester B. Pearson
Pierre Trudeau
Joe Clark
John Turner
Brian Mulroney
Kim Campbell
Jean Chretien
Paul Martin

WWW.FIVERIVERSPUBLISHING.COM

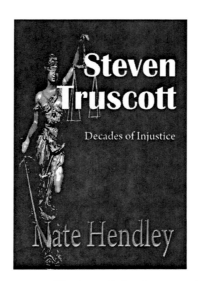

Steven Truscott: Decades of Injustice

by Nate Hendley
ISBN 9781927400210
eISBN 9781927400227
Trade paperback, 6 x 9, 128 pages
November 1, 2012

Imagine being a 14 year-old boy who takes a classmate on a bike ride one spring evening. In the days to follow, the classmate is found dead and you stand accused of rape and murder. There's no direct physical evidence tying you to the crime, but that doesn't matter. In a lightning fast trial you are convicted and sentenced to death. As far as the press and public are concerned, you are guilty and deserve to die. Such was the fate of Steven Truscott, living with his family on an army base in small-town Ontario in 1959. Read the shocking true story of a terrible case of injustice and the decades long fight to clear Truscott's name.

STONEHOUSE COOKS

by Lorina Stephens
ISBN 9780986642333
eISBN 9780986642364
Trade Paperback 6 x 9, 220 pages
August 1, 2011

Stonehouse Cooks offers recipes, meal plans and strategies to bring nutrition, delicious food and fun into the kitchen and on to the table. Lorina Stephens examines the real food revolution from both a modern and historical perspective, and offers guidance not only for the kitchen, but the barbecue and open-fire cookery. A perfect companion to *The Organic Home Garden,* by Patrick Lima.

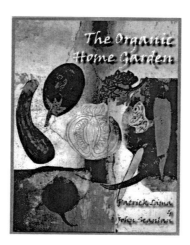

THE ORGANIC HOME GARDEN

by Patrick Lima and John Scanlan
ISBN 9780986542756
eISBN 9780986642357
Trade Paperback 7 x 10, 336 pages
June 7, 2011

In the *Organic Home Garden,* Patrick and John, take readers step-by-step through the engaging process of growing the best possible food — from spring's first spinach, asparagus and salad greens, through the summer abundance of tomatoes, cucumbers, melons and all, right into fall's harvest of squash, leeks, carrots and potatoes.

Often, a small timely tip makes all the difference, and this dynamic team leaves nothing out. Whether you tend a small city yard, a full-size country garden or something in between, their instructive, easy to follow and often humorous advice will ensure you make the very best use of the space you have — and you can't get any more local, seasonal and organic than food from your own yard.

Combine this with John's unique and vibrant artistic paintings, and you have a book that stands out from the wall of glossy, manufactured gardening publications, making

The Organic Home Garden a stand-alone, stand-out book sure to intrigue and capture gardeners, artists and customers who conduct their lives to a different rhythm. A perfect companion for Lorina Stephens' *Stonehouse Cooks.*

Reading Patrick Lima's eloquent, practical The Organic Home Garden *is like having a mentor stand beside us as we sow and reap.*— Betty Fox *Garden Making Magazine*

CPSIA information can be obtained at www.ICGtesting.com
Printed in the USA
LVOW07s0759040315

429141LV00011B/137/P